THE HEALING CONNECTION

HEAVEN'S HEALTH CARE PLAN

BRAD H. SPENCER

Publisher's Name: Brad H. Spencer
ISBN: 978-1-962142-59-5

Dedication

I dedicate this book in memory of my grandmother, Katherine C. Spencer. A godly woman who took me in when she didn't have to, showered me with unconditional love when I was unlovely, believed in me when others did not, and prayed for me that I might know her Lord and savior. Her life was a legacy of love.

Endorsements

From time to time there comes a fresh sound. This is one of those times. The book by Brad Spencer, *The Healing Connection,* is full of fresh thoughts from the Word of God.

When I first received the manuscript, I had no idea of the impact the book would have on me. Even as I began reading it, I assumed I would only skim over it. However, I soon realized I was underlining every other sentence, as well as rereading many pages. The anointing on the book is extraordinary. No, better said, it is supernatural!

Along with this tremendous book, I spent two days with Brad Spencer, witnessing miracle healing after miracle healing. I then realized I had to do all I could to help this special man share his great faith in God's power to heal with as many people as possible.

I heartily recommend *The Healing Connection,* and I encourage all that face bad health reports to get in touch with this anointed man for the prayer of faith. I thank God for Brad Spencer and the great gift of healing God has given him.

As I said, get ready for something fresh as you read.

John Avanzini

It has been my privilege to know Brad Spencer as a dear friend and fellow minister for many years. I sincerely believe that God has raised him up to bring the message of faith, hope and healing to His end times generation.

In *The Healing Connection,* Brad Spencer brings a sure word of revelation and instruction in the area of receiving and keeping our healing. He establishes very quickly in this book, that it is God's will to heal you and not His will for you to be sick. He very accurately and methodically proceeds to build upon this much attacked truth with the Word of God.

As long as we are in the world, Satan will continue to kill, steal and destroy; that is his assignment. As Brad so skillfully declares, if the body of Christ will attain this knowledge and walk in it, Satan's days of deceiving us are over.

Brad brings this truth with balance and confidence. This book will bring great blessing to those who read it and then put it into practice in their daily lives.

Louise Brock

It is with great honor that we provide an endorsement for the book, *The Healing Connection,* which you are about to read. This book has had a profound impact on our lives as well as our church and community. The content of this work will release faith, challenge your thinking, and revolutionize your concept of a loving Heavenly Father.

You will quickly recognize this to be a discipleship tool for all those who have a born again experience. Clarity will come regarding healing as a foundational understanding of the Kingdom.

We always recommend people to have multiple copies to liberally sow into the lives of others.

Pastor Brad speaks directly and clearly; with no guile. Having known Brad on a personal basis, his only motive for this work is love. Read this with great expectancy!! The Holy Spirit will certainly confirm this message to your heart. Be blessed with what you are about to read. This will be an "altar stone" experience.

Pastors Jim & Jill Chapin
Living Word Christian Center

Testimonial

This is a testimony mailed to me a few weeks after conducting a healing service at a church I ministered at.

"I stand in awe of God and His promises for us, His children. I would like to share with you what happened to my daughter when you prayed over her.

You were at our church on April 13, 2008. My daughter went up for a healing in her spine. She was diagnosed at age 13 with scoliosis.

I work for three orthopedic surgeons. I am an X-ray technologist with 30 years' experience, so you know I have seen a lot of curvatures of the spine as well as many other conditions.

I would like to explain to you what her physical appearance looked like. At age 13 I noticed her right shoulder rested much higher than her left. She also started to complain about soreness and stiffness in the middle of her spine, known as the thoracic area. Also, there was a very large hump on the right of her thoracic spine.

I took her to our family physician, and he gave me a requisition to either go to our local hospital or I could take the X-rays myself at the facility I work at. I chose to make an appointment with one of the surgeons at work and to take the X-rays myself.

The doctor looked at the x-rays, told me her curves were 43° in the lumbar and I believe 38° in the thoracic. The primary curve was in her lumbar spine. He told me that I had two choices; take her to Cleveland or Pittsburg where he knows surgeons at both facilities.

We chose Pittsburgh and started the long process of treatment. The first thing the doctor said the very first time we met him was 'I could operate on her spine today, it's that bad.' This did not leave a good impression. I chose the conservative route of a back brace. My daughter would have needed 4 rods: 2 sets total in her spine. There would have been two in the thoracic and two in the lumbar.

We went through two braces and were going on out third brace when she stopped growing. She had to wear the brace 23 hours a day; the one hour without it was to shower. She did this for three years and now just at night until age 18.

The last doctor's appointment was August of 2007, and the report was discouraging. The only thing the doctor said was that her head was centered to her spine and her curves were balanced at 30° each.

She came up April 13, 2008, expecting from God. When you laid hands on her, the curves in her spine burned and stayed that way for 24 hours. Monday night I had her bend over and the large hump on her back was almost completely flat, her ribs under her sternum on the right side and the hump have gone down significantly. Since April 13, 2008, she has grown 1 ½ inches. She is 20 years old and has not grown since she was 16. What God did in 24 hours the back brace could not do in 5 years. May God be glorified!" Grateful Mom in PA

Testimonial

I am writing this to acknowledge how much encouragement this book, The Healing Connection meant to me when I had lost hope and was even saving money to bury myself. Two MD's had told me I had cancer and it had spread to both breasts. My energy was fading fast. I put myself on prayer lists to be prayed for. Another pastor sent me Pastor Brad's book, The Healing Connection. I read this book every day to give me hope and encouragement, and I prayed that Father God would heal me. I am healed of cancer today! I am also grateful for Pastor Brad's book, which gave me encouragement to believe. It is the best book on healing I have ever read

MC in California

Contents

FOREWORD

The purpose of this book is twofold: 1) to teach you the principles that govern the kingdom of God, 2) to teach you how to live a long life satisfied, even though you may have been told by a doctor that you have a short time to live.

Many have been gloriously saved from the kingdom of darkness. But after conversion they have been abandoned and have not been taught how to live the Christian life. We read in the New Testament about all the wonderful miracles and how healing was brought to many by the Lord and His disciples. Yet, we've been told that healing and many of God's promises are not for today. It is sad to think that ministers of the gospel have contributed to this error and robbed the saints of God from their covenant benefits.

If you have a "so-called" incurable disease, this book is for you. It makes no difference whether you have cancer, a brain tumor or even AIDS; through Father God's healing provision you can live! I realize that I just made a very bold statement, but if you will do your part, then you'll soon discover that God has already done His part concerning His healing provision.

Before we go any further, I want you to understand that "faith" is a lifestyle. It's not a magic wand or just something you seek after when you find a mountain in your life. It is possible to obtain physical healing in a short period of time, but if you have a death sentence hanging over your head then you have much to learn and no time to waste. You may have faithfully attended church over the years, but you may have been taught incorrectly. So, realize that it takes time to learn new things as it also takes time to unlearn some old things.

You and I each have a role to play in your healing. Mine is to teach you the principles of the kingdom of God and how they operate. Your role is to learn and appropriate God's healing provision. I'm going to say some things that may challenge your thinking and doctrines, possibly upset you or even rattle your cage so to speak. If that happens just remember this: if the doctor's report states that you are going to die, then what do you have to lose?

Let's get started and begin our journey through the scriptures and answer the questions you may have, concerning the promised provision of God's healing power!

CHAPTER ONE

IS IT GOD'S WILL FOR ME TO BE HEALED?

You are not the only one who has asked this question. Thousands upon thousands down through history have wondered as well. Let's look at a man who asked Jesus this same question almost two thousand years ago and got an answer. The account is found in Matthew 8:1-3 and is about a man who was condemned with the dreaded disease of leprosy:

"And when He was come down from the mountain, great multitudes followed Him. And behold, a leper came to Him, and bowed down to Him, saying, "Lord, if You are willing, You can make me clean." And He stretched out His hand and touched him, saying, "I am willing; be cleansed." And immediately his leprosy was cleansed."

Like many believers today, this man believed Jesus was able to heal him, but he was not sure whether He was willing. Jesus answered the leper by saying, "I am willing." This is amazing because of three reasons:

First, if Jesus was willing to heal that man, then He must be willing to heal all who are sick, or He would change from His position of willingness. The Bible clearly states in Malachi 3:6 *"For I am the Lord, I change not."*

Second, we find in 2 Chronicles 19:7 that God is not partial to anyone, *"Now then let the fear of the Lord be upon you; be very careful what you do, for the Lord our God will have no part in unrighteousness, or partiality, or the taking of a bride.* " God does not esteem one person above another. What Jesus did for that leper, He will do for you.

Third, Hebrews 13:8 states *"Jesus is the same yesterday, today and forever."* This tells us even though this healing took place nearly two thousand years ago, time does not alter the ability or the willingness of the Lord. What He did yesterday, He will do today!

Let's look at another scripture found in 3 John 1:2: *"Beloved, I pray that in all respects you may prosper and be in good health, just as your soul prospers."* What God is saying here is it is his greatest desire that you not only prosper in material things and in your soul or understanding, but also that you prosper in physical health! I understand death is appointed unto every man, but not until you have fulfilled the number of your days. We see this truth in Psalm 91:16: *"With long life will I satisfy him and show him my salvation."* Notice He did not say with a short life satisfied, or with a long life of suffering, but a LONG LIFE SATISFIED!

Many Bible teachers today have shackled the minds of Christians with statements such as the following: "Healing has passed away," or "God uses sickness in order to teach us something," and "Our suffering is bringing glory to God." These declarations are nothing more than religious nonsense! Let's use a commonsense approach to these kinds of statements and see whether they enhance or insult our intelligence.

THE SICKNESS THEORY

- If sickness glorifies God, then Jesus robbed the Father of His Glory by healing those who are sick.
- If sickness were the will of God, then our ways are higher than His ways and our thoughts than His thoughts because no caring and loving parent would put sickness on their own children.
- If sickness were the will of God, then it would be a sin to go to a doctor or druggist to obtain relief from pain and sickness.
- If sickness were the will of God, then Jesus would have gone about destroying the works of the Father rather than the works of the devil.
- If sickness were the will of God, then God would be recognized as the greatest criminal of all time and condemned to prison for child abuse.
- If sickness were the will of God, then every doctor and nurse would be a law breaker before God, and every hospital a house of rebellion.
- If sickness were the will of God for our instruction, then we would be obligated to use our faith to receive the worst of sickness and disease in order that we might learn.
- If sickness were the will of God for our instruction, then every believer would be a spiritual giant and graduate from life with honors at an early age.
- If sickness were the will of God for our instruction, then why do we not see the body of Christ learning? Either God's method is not effective, or we are simply incapable of learning.
- If sickness were placed on us for our instruction, then it should be automatically removed once God is satisfied

that we have learned our lesson.

- If sickness were placed on us for our instruction, then we should desire to be sick so that we can utilize the education system of God.
- If sickness were the will of God, then Jesus would have been lying when He said, "I do the things I see the Father doing," because He healed the sick.
- If sickness were the will of God, then God Himself would be sick; because Jesus taught His disciples to pray that the will of God be done on earth just as it is in heaven.
- If sickness were the will of God placed on us for our benefit, then God would have violated our freedom of choice. Should He not take it a step further and cause us all to be saved for our own benefit?
- If sickness were the will of God, then the human body is cursed with an immune system that constantly fights against the will of God.
- If sickness were the will of God, then Satan would be seen as a friend and rewarded for his service to the body of Christ.
- If sickness were the will of God, then we should rejoice when we hear that someone is dying with sickness and disease rather than offer them sympathy.

Do you see how foolish it is to say that God puts sickness on us or that it may not be God's will for us to be healed? What we need to do is employ good common sense. Please understand, negatives do not produce positives. I understand in an adverse situation you can get God involved through faith. But to say God is doing bad things in our lives to get a positive result is ignorance in the highest form.

All we need to do is look at what God said in James 1:17 *"Every good thing bestowed and every perfect gift is from above, coming*

***down from the Father of lights, with whom there is no variation,
or shifting shadow."*** The good and perfect gifts come from
heaven. If God puts sickness and disease on people, then we need
to start calling diseases "good gifts." Have you ever seen a good
and perfect cancer? How about a good and perfect heart attack?
I'm sure you've seen a good and perfect case of HIV or AIDS. Get
the point? We've been lied to by the kingdom of darkness through
pastors and teachers.

CHAPTER TWO

WHY DOES GOD ALLOW SICKNESS?

To answer this question, let's go back to the beginning. We need to get an understanding of where sickness and disease originated. God created earth as the habitation for his prized creation, mankind. Adam was created in the likeness and image of God. God then delegated authority and dominion to Adam in order to rule the earth under His own authority. Genesis 1:28 states, *"And God blessed them, and God said unto them, be fruitful, and multiply, and replenish the earth, and subdue it: and have dominion over the fish of the sea, and over the fowl of the air, and over every living thing that moves upon the earth."*

In a sense, the earth was leased to Adam. The earthly habitation was perfect and complete. No evil, sin, or sickness was found in the paradise God created until Adam bowed his knee to the outlaw angel, we call Satan and committed high treason before God. The rebellion unleashed sin into the earth and handed the authority, as well as the earth lease over to God's enemy. There was no sickness in the garden until sin came. So, it's easy to see that sickness is the offspring of its parent, sin.

Now, by looking at two references, let's prove the point that Satan gained the lease:

First, look at 2 Corinthians 4:4 that states, *"In whom the god of this world hath blinded the minds of them which believe not, lest the light of the glorious gospel of Christ, who is the image of God."* Satan is referred to here as the god of this world, or world order of things. He does not own the earth; he just rules the world system until the time that the lease runs out. This is why we have chaos, famines, floods, tornadoes, destruction, corruption, and disease in the world today. Negative things are automatic because of the influence of the kingdom of darkness.

Secondly, Jesus Himself bears witness to the fact that the earth was subleased when He Himself was tempted by the devil. Let's consider Luke 4:5-7: *"And the devil, taking him up into a high mountain, shewed unto him all the kingdoms of the world in a moment of time and the devil said unto him, all this power will I give thee, and the glory of them: for that is delivered unto me; And to whomever I will give it to. If thou therefore wilt worship me, all shall be thine."* Who delivered the kingdoms of this world over to Satan? Adam did in the garden of Eden.

I once heard a minister say that the devil was lying about possessing the kingdoms of this world. Well, if he were lying, then I believe Jesus would have known it and would have corrected him. And if it were a lie, then how would we be able to say Jesus was tempted in all like manner as we are, and yet without sin? Jesus was tempted, and Satan was correct in stating he held the lease until the time that it runs out. Having said all this, let's put the question in proper perspective: God allows sickness and disease in the earth not because it is His will but because of Adam's treason and fall from grace.

We also need to understand that God gave us a will or created us as free moral agents in the earth. This means He will allow what you and I will allow. You see, your flesh gives you authority on this planet. The only way Satan could challenge Adam and Eve for the right to rule this world's system was to borrow the flesh of a serpent. He did so because he didn't have one. If you do not believe that your flesh gives you authority in the earth, then see what kind of authority you have on earth after you die. So, flesh gives you both the right and the freedom of choice. When choice is coupled with the knowledge of the Word of God, it becomes a powerful force. Once this is achieved, then the Kingdom of darkness is no match for you!

Although Satan gained the earth's lease, Jesus did for us what we could not do for ourselves in that He ratified the Abrahamic covenant of faith with His own shed blood. He whipped the devil, stripped him, defeated him, and made a show of him openly. Jesus made you and me more than conquerors! This means we must enforce Satan's defeat through the authority in the name of Jesus. To prove this, I want to point out a conversation that Jesus had with His disciples which is recorded in Matthew 16:13-19:

"When Jesus came into the coasts of Caesarea Philippi, He asked his disciples saying, whom do men say that I the Son of man is? And they said, some say that thou art John the Baptist: some, Elias; and others, Jeremiah or one of the prophets. He saith unto them, but whom say ye that I am? And Simon Peter answered and said, Thou art the Christ, the Son of the living God. And Jesus answered and said unto him, blessed art thou, Simon Barjona: for flesh and blood hath not revealed it unto thee, but my Father which is in heaven. And I say also unto thee, that thou are Peter, and upon this rock I will build my church; and the gates of hell shall not prevail against it. And I will give unto thee the keys of the kingdom of heaven: and whatsoever thou shalt bind on earth shall be bound in heaven: and whatsoever thou shalt loose on earth shall be loosed in heaven."

I'm sure you have heard quite a few St. Peter jokes in the past. But some religious groups actually believe that Peter is the keeper of the pearly gates in heaven. Nothing could be further from the truth. What Jesus is saying is Peter's response to the question of Jesus's identity was revelation from the Father. On the rock of revelation Jesus is building the church and the power of the kingdom of darkness cannot -- and will not -- prevail against it. That's because the church, not Peter, has been given the keys of the kingdom. Jesus is not referring to the Kingdom that it is to come; he is referring to the Kingdom that abides within us through the new birth.

Let's look at Romans 14:17: *"For the kingdom of God is not meat and drink; But righteousness, peace and joy in the Holy Ghost."* This is not referring to the physical kingdom that is to come. If it were, then we would not have the correct standing with God at this present time.

Go back to an earlier reference, Matthew 6:9-10, in which Jesus taught His disciples to pray: *"After this manner therefore pray ye: Our Father which art in heaven, hallowed be thy name. Thy kingdom come, Thy will be done in earth, as it is in heaven."* Jesus taught His disciples to pray that the kingdom come because when it comes, the will of God can be done on earth as it is in heaven.

Jesus later stated in Luke 17:21, *"nor will they say, 'Look, here it is!' or, 'there it is!' For behold, the kingdom of God is within you."* The good news is the kingdom of God is within us through the new birth!

The Jews were looking for a conquering Messiah and missed the spiritual Kingdom the atoning Messiah came to establish. Understand that you were made the righteousness of God in Christ Jesus. The keys that have been given are for this life and not the one to come. A key in the natural gives you entrance into something, so the keys of the kingdom of God give you entrance into the principles that govern God's kingdom.

Notice the first key has to do with binding. He is referring to the works of the enemy or things you don't desire. Be aware that God is not going to bind the works of the enemy. We have to do that, or nothing will be done about it.

The second key has to do with the loosening or obtaining something that we desire concerning God's promised provision. Let me say again if something is going to be bound or loosed in your life, you will have to do it because you have the keys. God's part is done. He's done all He's ever going to do about your healing. It's time for you to do your part by binding the curse of sickness and disease and loosening God's provision of healing power in your life. Some have learned through wrong teaching that God is going around healing some and not others and that we as believers have nothing to do with whether or not we are healed. I want to point out a reference to you that will expose the ignorance that is in that belief:

And coming to His hometown He began teaching them in their synagogue, so that they became astonished, and said, "Where did this man get this wisdom, and these miraculous powers?" is not this the carpenter's son? Is not His mother called Mary and His brothers, James and Joseph and Simon and Judas?" And His sisters are they not all with us? Where then did this man get all these things?" And they took offense at Him. But Jesus said to them, "A prophet is not without honor except in his hometown, and in his own household." And He did not do many miracles there because of their unbelief.

(Matthew 13:54-58)

Notice Jesus could have done mighty miracles in His hometown. Something hindered Him from doing so. What was it? It was familiarity with Him that caused them not to believe. Unbelief kept the provision of God's healing power from flowing in their lives, just as is does today. Isn't that sad? The people looked at Jesus in the natural and became offended at Him even though they acknowledged His wisdom and miraculous powers. They limited Jesus to the degree that He could not do miracles for them because they chose not to believe. Unbelief does not limit God, but unbelief will limit what God can do in your life.

CHAPTER THREE

I'M CONVINCED SO FAR, BUT HOW DOES IT WORK?

It works by faith. Faith is a creative force that abides in the Word of God. Romans 10:17 declares, *"So faith comes by hearing, and hearing by the word of God."* If faith comes by hearing the Word, then there must be faith in the Word to cause each promise to come to pass or become tangible in this physical realm.

Romans 12:3 teaches us that God has given to everyone the measure of faith. So how do we measure how much faith we have? By how much of the Word we have abiding on the inside of us. We could say that the Word of God would be the total source of Bible faith. For instance, Romans 10:9 says, *"if you confess with your mouth the Lord Jesus, and believe in your heart that God raised Him from the dead, you shall be saved."* There would be sufficient faith in that verse for someone to be saved; however, faith to be healed would not be found in Romans 10:9. We need to understand what this verse is saying concerning the operation of faith.

The creative force of faith is twofold: confessing and believing. Romans 10:10 says, *"For with the heart man believes, resulting in righteousness, and with the mouth he confesses, resulting in salvation."* You may be thinking this sounds like "name it and claim it, confess it and possess it." Well, that's exactly what it is. It is the way God operates. Romans 4:17 states: *"as it is written, a father of many nations have I made you in the sight of Him whom he believed, even God, who gives life to the dead and calls into being that which does not exist."* By faith, God calls for what

He doesn't have so it will manifest into this natural realm.

Now before you go any further, we need to understand that faith does not call things that are, as though they are not. But rather, faith calls things that are not as though they were. Some have gone under the banner of faith and denied the existence of a particular sickness or disease. That is not faith. That is living in denial! Faith calls for what it does not have as a manifested fact. Let's say that a person is diagnosed with a brain tumor, and he declares that he believes that the tumor is not there by faith. The truth is the tumor does exist. If sickness did not exist, then God would have no reason to supply healing. Faith wouldn't deny the existence of the tumor but would deny the tumor the right to exist in the body. Then faith would call for what didn't exist and that would be healing. Faith would call for healing power to come and perfect a healing and a cure within the person and not stop until they are completely made whole. That's what faith would do.

Let me give you a personal example. Several years ago, I was doing some remodel work and stepped off a ladder onto a hammer lying on the floor. I fell off and landed on my left foot and immediately realized I had broken my foot. It immediately swelled and the pain was severe. I said to the person with me, "I broke my foot." He said, "I wouldn't confess that." I responded by saying, "It's either broken or it isn't. If it is broken, saying that it's not broken won't change the present fact. But I declare in the name of Jesus that healing power flows throughout my foot and perfects a healing and a cure and will not stop until its completely made whole." This happened on a Thursday evening. I called a member of our church, who is a podiatrist and explained what had happened. He suggested that I come to his office for an x-ray. The x-ray proved that I had indeed broken my foot. He started to place a cast on my foot, and I told him, "No way," because I would be preaching on my foot in the Sunday morning services. Think about it, I would have had to wear that thing for six to eight weeks!

Knowing that I wouldn't permit a plaster cast, the good doctor suggested a removable splint with what I called "designer" shoe and a commitment to keep it on until Sunday morning. I agreed to this since the splint and shoe were not a hindrance to my faith at all. You see, doctors and medicine aid the natural healing of the human body, or they put something in the body or take something out. They are not healers; God is the healer! My trust and confidence was in the Word, not in man's ability. Please don't misunderstand me. I thank God for doctors and nurses. They believe in healing when you cannot get most preachers to.

For the next two days everyone I saw asked, "what happened to your foot?" I replied, "I broke my foot. Even though you can't see it, healing power is flowing through my foot and will not stop until it's completely mended- in Jesus' name." You see, I didn't deny the existence of the problem. I just called for what I didn't have and that was a healed foot. On Sunday morning, as I had promised my doctor, I removed the splint, and my foot was perfectly healed! Less than three days, the Word had done its work. Sure beats 6 to 8 weeks, doesn't it?

Let's consider what the apostle Paul had to say about calling things that are not: *"For momentary, light affliction is producing for us an eternal weight of glory far beyond all comparison," (2 Corinthians 4:17).* If we look at this verse by itself, we can gain insight as to why many Bible teachers believe we are to suffer the afflictions of this life. They think that by suffering we are storing up blessings in heaven. Well, the verse almost seems to indicate such a belief until we look at the following verse 2 Corinthains 4:18: *"while we look not at the things which are seen, but at*

14

the things which are not seen; for the things which are seen our temporal, but the things which are not seen are eternal." It says that while we look not or choose not to consider the present afflictions, we should look to the things that we do not see. Your circumstance is nothing more than the circle you are standing in. Rather than focusing on your present circle, draw a new one and start seeing what Father God sees.

People stumble in regard to faith because they want to receive from God through their five senses. They say believing in what you don't see doesn't make sense. They're right! It doesn't and it's not supposed to! The five senses are not designed to operate in the spirit world. That is why God gave us faith. Faith will make a connection between you and the healing provision that is in heaven and cause it to manifest in the physical, thus bypassing your five senses.

There is no power to change what you have by focusing on and declaring what you have. The power to change what you have is in saying and declaring God's solution to your problem. 2 Corinthians 4:18 also says that things which are seen are temporal while things that are not seen are eternal. If you're sick, what is it that is not seen? Healing! If you are discouraged, what is it that is not seen? Hope! Sickness and disease may be temporary conditions in your life, but healing is eternal. The afflictions of this life only work an eternal weight of glory when you look not at the things you see such as sickness in your body.

As I said earlier, this is the way God operates. Isaiah 46:10 says God declares the end from the beginning. This means He declares that which He desires and the thing that He desires becomes tangible. Faith always gets what it calls for. In Genesis 1:2-3, we find that God looked over the earth and saw there was darkness.

If He called it as He saw it - - the way most believers do - - He would have said it was dark and getting darker. But no, He called for what He didn't have and said, "Light be," and glory to God, light came! Even God doesn't like to work in the dark!

Now let's look at some examples of what Jesus had to say about calling things that are not: in Luke 17:11-14, ten lepers cried out to Jesus for mercy. He told them to show themselves to the priest to confirm their healing and while on the way they were cleansed. They were as leprous as ever when they started off. What was Jesus doing? He was calling ten lepers clean. Notice also that while "on the way" the miracle happened.

In John 2:1-10 Jesus visited a wedding in Cana. The wedding party had run out of wine. Jesus told the servants to fill six water pots with water, draw out some and give it to the headwaiter. By the time it got to the headwaiter it had become wine. What was Jesus doing? He was calling water wine. He had water; what He wanted was wine. Notice again that nothing happened while they did nothing, but rather the physical manifestation came while they were "on the way" or when they acted on their faith.

In John 4:46-53, a royal official entreated Jesus to come heal his son who was at the very point of death. Jesus said, "Go your way; your son lives." The man believed the Word that Jesus spoke and started off. His servant met him and said his son was healed. Jesus called a sick son healed!

In Mark's gospel, chapter eleven, Jesus went to the fig tree to see if He could find any fruit, but He found nothing. He declared that no one would eat from it again. While passing by the next morning, the disciples noticed the fig tree was dried up from the roots. What was Jesus doing? He was calling a live fig tree dead!

Do you get the point? It's all through the Book. Calling things that are not or placing a demand on the promised provision of God, is the way Jesus and Father God operate.

" Well, if that's the way you believe, stay away from elevators! If the elevator is on the third floor and you're on the first, you'll have to take the stairs. Because if you push the button, you are calling for what you don't have. You will also have to stay away from telephones as well. Because, if you dial someone's number, then you are calling for what you do not have. Faith is as simple as calling the dog. If the dog is not there – call it! The creation of God is designed to respond to words. It amazes me that people call for what they don't have all the time in the natural. But when it concerns the things of God, they become religious and say ignorant things such as, "Stay away from that naming and claiming stuff.

CHAPTER FOUR

THE POWER OF WORDS

In our last chapter, we left off talking about Jesus cursing the fig tree. He used this as an illustration to teach His disciples how the kingdom of God operates. In Marks Gospel chapter 11:22-23 Jesus sad, *"Have faith in God."* The literal Greek language says, "Have or operate in the God kind of faith!" God has placed His faith, the same faith He used when He created the world, in His Word. You may question whether or not we can have the God kind of faith. But remember that Galatians 2:20 states that we live by faith of the Son of God. Let's look at Mark 11:23:

> *"For verily I say unto you, that whosoever shall say unto this mountain, be thou removed, and be thou cast into the sea; and shall not doubt in his heart but shall believe those things which he saith shall come to pass; he shall have whatsoever he saith."*

There are five things that I want to point out about the God kind of faith.

1. **JESUS SAID YOU HAD TO TALK TO YOUR MOUNTAIN.** A mountain symbolizes a problem in your life. You might say, "I don't believe in talking to my problems." Yes, you do. You do it all the time, but you do not realize it. I often hear people say, "I'll never get over this mountain; the mountain is big and getting bigger." That is talking to your mountain. There is a song that has been out for several years, and the lyrics are: "Lord don't move that mountain, just give me strength to climb." Now that is ignorant and embalmed with religious

error! I've seen people sing that song with tears streaming down their face. First of all, Jesus does not move our mountains; we do. He said for you to speak to the mountain and command it to be removed and it, the mountain - the problem, will obey you. Stop trying to climb mountains that God intended for you to move by speaking faith filled words.

In the Old Testament book of Zachariah, Zerubbabel was one of the exiles who chose to return to Jerusalem to rebuild the temple. The mountain that he and others faced was to awaken Israel from their indifference and complete the work. If you've ever worked with people, you know what a challenge, or mountain, that can be. An angel brought to Zerubbabel the Word of the Lord and how to move the mountain. Let's examine God's method:

"Then he answered and spoken to me, saying, this is the word of the Lord unto Zerubbabel, saying, not by might, nor by power, but by my spirit the Lord of hosts. Who art thou, O great mountain? Before Zerubbabel thou shalt become a plain: and he shall bring forth the headstone thereof with shouting, crying, grace, grace unto it." (Zechariah 4:6-7)

God instructed Zerubbabel to shout "Grace" to the mountain. This makes sense if you understand that grace is God's willingness to use his power and ability on our behalf. Your attitude should be: "what is the mountain of sickness standing before me? Mountain, I command you in the name of Jesus to move!" Remember: if you do not move the mountain, the mountain will move you.

2. **SAY WHAT YOU DESIRE.** The greatest problem most people have is directly under their nose. It is their mouth.

They constantly talk the problem. They say things are bad and getting worse. We'll never pay off these debts. This sickness will be the death of me yet.

Jesus never spoke things He did not desire; He always spoke the desired result. One of the most profound scriptures in the Bible is found in Proverbs 18:21: *"death and life are in the power of the tongue: and they that love it shall eat the fruit thereof."* Words are containers; they contain either faith or fear. Faith and fear are the same in definition but opposite in principle. Both believe that what you cannot see will come to pass. Fear will cause what you don't desire to gravitate towards you, such as the curses of life. Faith on the other hand will cause what you do desire to gravitate toward you. Fear is confidence in the curses of life while faith is confidence in the words of God.

Many people like to associate their mountain with Job's troubles. What they don't understand is that Job said, "What I greatly feared has come upon me." Everything Job feared came to pass in his life. When Job repented, God was the one who restored to him twofold all he had lost. If you're going to identify with Job, identify with his restoration and not his fear.

Jesus quoted the Old Testament where it states, "The testimony of two is true." When you agree with what the devil said, you will get what you and he have agreed on. But if you agree with God and what He said in His Word, you will get what He said. It always amazes me that Christians are quick to hear the voice of the enemy and agree with what he has said but are slow to hear the voice of God and agree with what God has said about them. I make it a point in life to never allow the devil to speak to me. Why would I want to listen to the father of lies? Jesus never spoke what he didn't desire. He always spoke the desired result. Realize the words coming out of your mouth are producing either death or life. If you accept and talk about the death sentence placed over your head, then death will come. Wouldn't it be better to rise up and speak the words that will produce a long life satisfied? Sure, it would!

3. **DOUBT NOT IN YOUR HEART.** Many years ago while attending Rema Bible Training Center, I heard Kenneth E. Hagin make this statement: "When you're tempted to doubt, doubt your doubts. Don't doubt the Word of God." There is much wisdom in that statement. Doubt is nothing more than false information challenging the truth of the Word. James 1:5-7 says:

"If any of you lack wisdom, let him ask of God, that giveth to all men liberally, and upbraideth not; and it shall be given to him. But let him ask in faith, nothing wavering. For he that waverth is like a wave of the sea driven with the wind and tossed. For let not that man think that he shall receive anything from the Lord."

Now can you see why so many prayers have not been answered for the body of Christ? They pray in doubt and unbelief. When their prayers don't get answered, they alter the Word of God to fit their circumstances, instead of altering their circumstances to fit the Word of God. That means when they don't do what it takes to receive their healing, they blame it on God and say that it must have not been His will or that perhaps He has another plan. If a sinner does not do what it takes to receive salvation, can we say that God has another plan? The only other plan would be the lake of fire! We need to stop being irresponsible and do what it takes to be healed just as we did what it took to be saved. Let's look at the classic example of someone who launched out in faith but fell because he doubted:

"And when the disciples saw Him walking on the sea, they were troubled, saying, it is a spirit; and they cried out for fear. But straightaway Jesus spoke unto them, saying, be of good cheer; it is I; be not afraid. And Peter answered him and said, lord, if it be thou, bid me come unto thee on the water. And he said, come. And when Peter was come down out of the ship, he walked on the water, to go to Jesus. But when he saw the wind boisterous, he was afraid; and beginning to sink, he cried, saying, Lord, save me. And immediately Jesus stretched forth his hand, and caught him, and said unto him, O thou of little faith, wherefore didst thou doubt?" (Matthew 14:26-31)

When Peter saw it was Jesus walking on the water, he said, "Lord if its you, command me to come to you." What could Jesus say? "It's not me?" Jesus said, "Come." Peter got out of the boat and started walking on the water. But notice that the wind and waves got his attention away from Jesus and onto his present circumstances. Peter was walking on water! But noticed that when he doubted, doubt nullified the effect of his faith and Peter began to sink. This is a common problem that people face; the five senses. Sensory perception was given to us that we might operate in this physical realm. Faith was given to us that we might operate in the Spirit realm. Confusion is the result when you attempt to see or feel the promise of healing before you believe. Doubt is the enemy of faith and will always cause you to sink as Peter did. Remember: always doubt your doubts, not the word.

4. **BELIEVE WHAT YOU SAY.** It has always amazed me that

a believer with a death sentence hanging over his head will come to church and testify that he is standing on God's word and believes that he is healed. Yet a short time later he dies and goes on to be with the Lord. Now almost everyone in the church is wondering why he was not healed. I can answer that question. What he said in church was not what he really believed. What he really believed is what he said to his spouse on the way home from church. What he really believed is what he said on the phone when his mama called. When mama said, "Child, how are you doing?" He replied, "Momma, I don't know what I'm going to do. It's bad and getting worse. I guess I need to go buy a burial plot." Now that's what he really believed! When you're in the battle, that's not the time to fall apart like a dollar watch. It's time to perform and do what you've been trained to do. It's time to stand with the shield of faith held high and quench all the fiery darts of the wicked one. Praise God!

In Mark's gospel, chapter nine, we find the account of Jesus coming down from the Mount of Transfiguration. He saw some religious leaders arguing with his disciples over a boy who was demon possessed. The father said to Jesus, "But if you can do anything, take pity on us and help us!" I like the way the New American Standard translates the response of Jesus. "If you can! All things are possible to him who believes." We found earlier that the leper in Matthew chapter eight believed that Jesus was able to heal him but wasn't sure whether He was willing. Here we have a man who questions the ability of Jesus. Let's get it straight: He is both able and willing. The real question is: Will you believe? Many today do not think they have a responsibility where their healing is concerned. So, I want to take you to the book of Matthew and look at the account of two blind men:

"And when Jesus departed thence, two blind men followed him, crying, and saying, Thou Son of David, have mercy on us. And when He came into the house, the blind men came to him: and Jesus saith unto them, believe ye that I am able to do this? They said unto Him, yes, Lord. Then touched be their eyes, saying, according to your faith be it unto you. And their eyes were opened; and Jesus straightly charged them, saying, see that no man know it." (Matthew 9:27-30)

Did you notice their faith had everything to do with whether they received healing for their blindness? Jesus said let it be done according to YOUR faith. Well, they must have had faith because their eyes opened. There was faith abiding in the words that Jesus spoke to them.

I've seen many blind eyes opened as I have traveled around the world conducting miracle and healing crusades. I remember one such meeting in Kenya, Africa. There was a twelve-year-old girl who was totally blind. While I was ministering to people through the laying on of hands, this little girl stated she had come for her healing. I noticed her eyes were milked over and fluid was draining from them. I began to weep just looking at her and I asked the Lord what he wanted me to do. I heard him say to me, "I want you to spit on her." I replied to him that I couldn't do any such thing as I hadn't spit on anyone since I had been saved. His response was that if I didn't obey, the little girl would not be healed. Well, not being well versed in the fine art of spitting, I spat in both of my hands, laid them over her eyes and she was instantly healed by the Lord. What a prime example of "believing is seeing!"

In January 1999, I was in a crusade in the city of Kakamega, Kenya. A woman brought up her two toddlers in the healing line. Again, I was instructed by the Lord to spit on my hands and place them on their eyes. God opened the blind eyes of those two small children. Because of this healing, large numbers of people in that woman's village have turned to the Lord! Isn't that just like our loving Heavenly Father?

5. **YOU CAN HAVE WHAT YOU SAY.** Having what you say is going to be the greatest revelation you've ever learned. Herein is the key that unlocks the door of provision that Jesus paid for with His own shed blood. In 1974, Brother Charles Capps of Arkansas was in Hickory, North Carolina for some meetings. During this time, God gave him one of the greatest reservations concerning Mark 11:23 that I have ever learned. God spoke to Brother Capps and said, "I told My people that they could have what they say, but My people are saying what they have." This revelation is so simple and yet profound! You see, there is no power in saying what you have, to change what you have. The power to change what you have is to have what you say. Or, as Brother Capps put it, "you can have what you say, or you can say what you have." I count it an honor to have such a revelation brought forth in the city where I pastor. I have made a commitment to the Lord that the teaching of faith and "having what you say" will emanate from this city into the entire world. Brother Capps returned to Hickory on April 22, 1977, and in that meeting, I was saved and filled with the Spirit. I will forever be grateful to Charles and Peggy Capps for their teaching and servitude to the body of Christ.

Now let's see if we can find anyone in the Word that believed in having what you say. *"And Elijah the Tishbite, who was of the inhabitants of Gilead, said unto Ahab, As the Lord God of Israel liveth before whom I stand, there shall not be dew nor rain these years, but according to my word."* (1 King

17:1) Imagine this - Elijah walked in before Ahab, the wicked king of Israel and declared that it was not going to rain until he said so! If you know the story, it didn't.

Let's see if the apostle Peter believed in having what you say: *"Then had the churches rest throughout all Judea and Galilee and Samaria and were edified; and walking in the fear of the Lord, and in the comfort of the Holy Ghost, were multiplied. And it came to pass, as Peter passed throughout all quarters, he came down also to the saints which dwelt as Lydda. And there he found a certain man named Aeneas, which had kept his bed eight years, and was sick of the palsy. And Peter said unto him, Aeneas, Jesus Christ maketh thee whole: arise, and make thy bed. And he arose immediately."* (Acts 9:32-34)

If Peter believed in saying what he had, he would have said, "Aeneas, I see you are paralyzed and will probably get worse." But no. Peter believed in having what he said. So, he said, "Aeneas, Jesus Christ heals you!"

Let's look at another reference. After all, Jesus said, "Let every fact be established out of the mouth of two or three witnesses." *"But Elymas the sorcerer for so is his name by interpretation withstood them, seeking to turn away the deputy from the faith. Then Saul, who also is called Paul, filled with the Holy Ghost, set his eyes on him, and said, O full of all subtlety and all mischief, wilt thou not cease to pervert the right ways of the Lord? And now, behold, the hand of the Lord is upon thee, and thou shalt be blind, not seeing the sun for a season. And immediately there fell on him a mist and darkness; and he went about seeking some to lead him by the hand."* (Acts 13:8-11)

Noticed that "having what you say" not only brings forth the provision of God that you desire, but it can also cause judgment to come. Imagine what the spiritual principle of faith can accomplish against sickness and disease!

CHAPTER FIVE

THE GUIDE WIRES TO FAITH

I'm sure you've noticed most utility poles have cables or wires that give support to the pole. Well faith works in much the same way. These guidewires are hope, love patience and works. Hope keeps faith expecting. Love keeps faith pure. Patience keeps faith content and works keeps faith activated. Let's examine them and see how they work as partners to the creative force of faith.

HOPE. *"Now faith is the substance of things hoped for, the evidence of things not seen."* Or we could say that faith gives substance to the things we hope for. (Hebrews 11:1). We need to begin with hope because faith gives substance to those things for which we hope. What things? Things or promises that you hope to receive from God's Word. You certainly could not believe to receive something that God did not promise in His Word. The Greek word for hope is elpizo (el-pid'-zo). It means confident expectation. According to Hebrews 11:1 Faith gives substance to things hoped for, therefore hope would be the blueprint to which the creative force of faith would give substance. The substance part would be the raw materials or components used to frame the project. We see this in verse three, where God said, *"By faith we understand that the worlds were framed by the Word of God."*

You see, God had a blueprint for the heavens which was the thing He hoped to accomplish or build. But hope was not enough in itself to cause this to come to pass. He needed a creative force that would give substance to, or frame, what He hoped to accomplish. The creative force is called faith.

That is what God did in Genesis 1:3 when He said: "Let there be light" and there was light. He hoped for light, but there wasn't any light until His faith brought forth the substance, we call light. This is how God created, or we would say "framed" the natural world in which we now live. Instead of calling for what they don't yet see, most Christians would declare that it's so dark we will never have any light.

We should see by now that hope is the starting point in receiving from God. I like to say it this way: Hope declares the promises are available to us; Faith declares they can be obtained right now! Hope in and of itself will not cause you to be healed. Many believers today are merely hoping to be healed. If you ask them in a healing line if they will be healed when you lay hands on them, they usually say, "I hope so." That is not faith; it's wishful fantasy. Bible Hope is the blueprint for your healing. Bible faith is the substance that believes to receive right now! You can walk in confidence if you know God position concerning His promises.

It angers me when I hear preachers declare that sometimes God says "No," to the healing request of His sons and daughters. There's a scripture that will help you understand God's position concerning His promises: *"For as many as may be the promises of God, in Him they are yes; wherefore also by Him is our Amen to the glory of God."* (2 Corinthians 1:20). You have most likely heard preachers say that God sometimes says "Yes," sometimes He says "No," and sometimes He says, "wait a while." Nothing could be further from the truth! Do you see a "no" in 2 Corinthians 1:20? Father God's response to His promises are always "yes." It's up to us to appropriate them by faith. The Word of God works when you work it – it won't if you don't.

You see friends, if the enemy can keep us ignorant concerning the promises of God and unsure of His willingness or ability, he'll keep us defeated. He does this through traditional religious teaching that says the promises are not for today. They passed away with the last apostle. Wouldn't it be sad to think that everything Jesus accomplished in the New Covenant passed away when the last apostle died? No, the Bible teaches us that Jesus is the same yesterday, today and forever. What Jesus did nearly two thousand years ago, He is still doing today, and I put my amen on that!

LOVE. Love is not just an attribute of God, for the Bible says that God IS love. In Galatians 5:6 we read, *"for in Christ Jesus neither circumcision nor uncircumcision means anything, but faith working through love."* Faith will not work apart from love. When we covered Mark 11:23 in our last chapter, we discovered that we CAN move mountains and have what we say if we believe and doubt not in our heart. But when Jesus taught about faith, He usually taught on forgiveness as well. That's right. If you're going to operate in the God kind of faith, you'll have to forgive people whom you hold grudges against, people who have offended you, and people who have hurt you.

I believe the greatest aspect of love is the ability to walk free from the snare of unforgiveness. Unforgiveness will shut down the effects of your faith and it will cause your prayer for healing to be hindered. Forgiveness is not a feeling; it's a faith decision.

Later on, I'll spend some time on how to forgive. But first let's see what the Bible says about walking in love towards others: *"If you forgive the sins of any, their sins have been forgiven them; if you retain the sins of any, they have been retained."* (John 20:22-23). Retaining the sins of others can hinder you in regard to your faith and keep you from the healing you need and desire. So be quick to forgive others and you will keep your side of the glass clean.

Even though we are to forgive others, it does not mean that we are required to have close fellowship with everyone. I think we often feel as if we have to be "buddies" in order to truly forgive. That could be the case in an area of restoration, but according to Amos 3:3 *"Can two walk together, except they be agreed?"*

There have been occasions when people have come to me and said I need to emphasize love more than faith. They say, "After all, faith works by love." I agree. But I also understand that love works by faith. With some people, you have to love them by faith! If you have unforgiveness towards someone, go to him and either forgive him or ask for forgiveness. Even if he refuses, you are free. I'm convinced that we must walk in forgiveness, but with some people it is better to love them from a distance.

Now let's talk about how to forgive others. In Luke 17:3-6 we read, *"Be on your guard! If your brother sins, rebuke him; and if he repents, forgive him. And if he sins against you seven times a day, and returns to you seven times, saying, "I repent," forgive him. And the apostles said to the Lord, "Increase our faith!" And the Lord said, "If you had faith like a mustard seed, you would say to the mulberry tree, 'be uprooted and be planted in the sea'; and it would obey you."*

I'm sure we could all forgive one offense in a day, but seven? The disciples must have felt the same way because they asked Jesus to increase their faith. Jesus couldn't do that because faith comes by hearing and hearing by the Word of God. But notice that Jesus said if you have faith as a seed you would say something. He's still dealing with the subject of forgiveness in this verse. What would faith as a seed say concerning forgiveness? It would say, "I choose to forgive." And every time that offense returns to your remembrance, it would say, "I have already forgiven and I'm not going to entertain thoughts of the past." Again, forgiveness is not a feeling.

Many times, we slip back into unforgiveness because we have thoughts concerning what someone did to us. Then we feel as if we didn't truly forgive them. Understand forgiveness is a decision that must be protected when we have a thought or someone else brings the memory of the past to our attention. Here's some food for thought from 1 Peter 4:8: *"Above all, keep fervent in your love for one another, because love covers a multitude of sins."* Also noticed that Jesus said we forgive our brother "if" he repents. Nowhere does the Bible instruct us to forgive people who refuse to repent or take personal responsibility. Until they do, we are simply to keep our hearts right towards them and walk in love.

PATIENCE. I'm convinced that we live in an instant society. Everybody wants instant coffee, instant food service and instant healing. There are times when one of the nine gifts of the Spirit, "gifts of healing and working of miracles," are in operation and we may see instant manifestations. But that is not always the case where faith is concerned. The characteristic of a miracle is that it is instant; the characteristic of a healing is that it is a recovery. Remember that believers lay hands on the sick - and they recover.

Several years ago, during a Wednesday night service in which I was ministering under the healing anointing, a couple brought up their five-year-old son to be ministered to. He had been born with two or more vertebrae missing in his back. Doctors had attempted bone grafting, but the procedure had failed and almost killed him. The child was left confined in a plastic body cast. Although I sensed the anointing on me when I had laid hands upon him, the boy did nothing but cry. There appeared to be no immediate change in his body. I told the parents that God's healing power was flowing in him and perfecting a healing and a cure within him.

About two weeks later, his father called me from Baptist Hospital in Winston-Salem, North Carolina, and told me that to the amazement of the doctors, the boy had grown the bones needed in his back. In fact, the doctor said that it would have been easier to grow a new spinal column rather than the vertebrae he needed. Here's a classic example of being patient. Understand that in many cases, healing is a process. Just as when you cut your finger, the body will begin the healing process.

Why is it so hard for some to imagine that God can heal things beyond that which the physical body can handle? I want you to see what God said about being patient: ***"that you may not be sluggish, but imitators of those who through faith and patience inherit the promises."*** (Hebrews 6:12). Notice that faith and patience work together. Some people give up on their healing right before it comes into manifestation. When you stand in faith, you should be prepared to stand forever and in doing so, you won't have to.

Patient is the time period between the planting of the seed and the harvesting of the crops. After the farmer plants his seed in the soil, he must then protect the seed from weeds, insects, weather, and drought. The same is true with the seed of God's Word. We must protect the Word sown from doubt, fear, and impatience. Just as surely as you have sown, you will reap if you do not quit.

I've had many people say to me, "Well Pastor, I'm praying for patience." My response is always, "What are you doing that for?" Patience is not something you pray for but something you must develop yourself in. Let's look at an example of that in the

Word: ***"But the fruit of the Spirit is love, joy, peace, patience, kindness, goodness, faithfulness..."*** (Galatians 5:22). Although the Word "spirit" is capitalized in this verse, it is not capitalized in the Greek language. The translators did that to indicate a reference to the Holy Spirit. The subject of this chapter is the re-created human Spirit. Understand that when you were born again, God placed His attributes into your spirit. So, you have within your spirit love, joy, peace, patience and so on. You do not need to pray for patience. But you must develop yourself in accordance to the fruit of patience that is within you by saying, "I am patient in every circumstance of life. Through faith and patience, I always inherit the promises of God!"

WORKS. *"What use is it, my brethren, if a man says he has faith, but he has no works? Can that faith save him? If a brother or sister is without clothing and in need of daily food, and one of you says to them, "Go in peace, be warmed and fulfilled," and yet you do not give them what is necessary for their body, what use is that? Even so faith, if it has no works, is dead, being by itself."* (James 2:14-17)

You cannot see the wind, but you can see the effects that the wind has on the elements around you. So, it is with faith. Your faith can be seen through your works. The final result being the tangible substance of what you believed to receive.

Faith must have corresponding action. This is where most people miss it. They testify that they believe they are healed but act as if they are still sick. They're talking faith in church but at the same time making provisions for failure. Don't misunderstand me. I'm not saying that you work for your healing; healing was paid for in the atonement. You simply allow not only what you say, but also what you do to be in line with what you believe. The same is true with salvation. The Bible says in Philippians 2:12, *"work out your salvation with fear and trembling."* It didn't say work for, but rather take the salvation that is within you and work it on the outside.

On Christmas Eve 1986, I experienced symptoms of the flu early in the afternoon. These symptoms didn't come gradually; they came suddenly and with great intensity. I remember falling onto the bed while quoting healing Scriptures such as, "Himself took my infirmities and carried away my diseases and by His stripes I am healed!"

Then I heard the Lord say, "Well, are you healed?" I answered, "Yes, Sir".

When I said that, the fever was still racing through my body. I still felt weak, and my joints ached. Then the Lord said to me, "well, It looks to Me like a healed man ought to be up and busy instead of lying in bed at 2 o'clock in the afternoon." I realized I was going to have to put my faith to work and act as if the Word was true because it is. With no immediate change in my circumstances, with great difficulty I got out of bed and decided that it was a good time to do spring cleaning in the month of December. About an hour later, I noticed that every symptom had left my body, and I had the manifestation of what I believed I received while lying in bed. Faith beats sickness any day of the week! Do you think it would have worked while I was lying in bed? I think not.

CHAPTER SIX

ACTING ON YOUR FAITH

This chapter will describe in more detail some of the things that we learned in the previous chapter concerning works. There is a story in the Word of God about a woman who was healed by applying the principles that we have been learning. Let me point out that the people who received their healing in the New Testament were not highly educated, nor were they of noble decent. They were people who took Jesus at his word and believed.

"And a certain woman which had an issue of blood twelve years, and had suffered many things of many physicians, and had spent all she had, and was nothing better, but rather grew worse," (Mark 5:25-26). According to Levitical law, a person with this kind of disease had to be quarantined from society. Think about the sorrow she felt during the twelve years that she was away from her family! The passage goes on to say that she went to every physician in the town and spent all her money, but she only grew worse. Such is the plight of many people today. This woman took four basic steps that caused her to be healed. Take note of these four easy principles that enabled her to receive the healing she so desired:

"When she had heard of Jesus, came in the press behind, and touched his garment. For she said if I may touch but his clothes, I shall be whole. And straightway the fountain of her blood was dried up; and she felt in her body that she was healed of that plague." (Mark 5:27-29)

SHE HEARD. Notice that she heard about Jesus. We've already discussed the fact that faith comes by hearing, and hearing by the Word of God (Romans 10:17). She heard the testimony of the demon possessed man who had lived among the tombs. Jesus told him to go and tell people the great deliverance that God had done for him. This testimony that she heard caused two things to come to her: hope and faith. This reminds me of what Peter said in Acts 10:38: **"You know of Jesus of Nazareth, how God anointed Him with the Holy Spirit and with power, and how he went about doing good, and healing all who were oppressed by the devil; for God was with him."** I want to point out here that it's not possible for God to have placed sickness and disease on the people that Jesus healed. If so, the scripture would have stated that Jesus went about healing all who were oppressed by God.

Many people today are held in bondage by the very things Jesus redeemed them from simply because they are ignorant of the truth. Traffic laws are not nullified on behalf of the offenders simply because they are ignorant of them; ignorance of the law is not a justifiable defense.

The same is true for spiritual laws. Jesus taught the importance of knowing the truth: *"Jesus therefore was saying to those Jews who had believed Him, 'If you abide in My word, then you are truly disciples of Mine; and you shall know the truth, and the truth shall make you free."* (John 8 31-32). If you have been given false information by past teachings, then you have heard wrong. If what you have heard is wrong, then what you're believing is wrong. If you're believing is wrong, then you do not have the truth and it is not possible for you to be free from the problems of life. It's always the truth that you know that sets you free!

SHE SAID. The spoken Word releases faith. 1 Peter 1:23

teaches us that we are born again by the incorruptible seed of God's Word. Jesus taught in the parable of the Sower that there are four types of soil, or conditions of the heart, into which the seed of the word is sown in. You and I are Sowers.

The way we sow is with the tongue, or with the words that we speak. Here's a good example of how this works: ***"Do not let kindness and truth leave you; bind them around your neck, write them on the tablet of your heart."*** (Proverbs 3:3). How do you write the Word on the tablet of your heart? Well, let's consider Psalm 45:1: ***"My heart overflows with a good theme; I address my verses to the King; my tongue is the pen of a ready writer."*** Glory to God, it's the tongue that pens the Word on the tablet of the heart! When we speak the Word, the Word gets deposited into your heart.

The heart is where you do your believing. Romans 10:10 says, ***"With the heart man believes."*** Isn't it wonderful that you can believe and still not figure everything out with your head? One of the most profound versus along this line is found in Psalm 77:6: ***"I call to remembrance my song in the night: I commune with mine own heart: and my spirit made diligent search."*** Made diligent search to do what? To cause to come to pass that which was spoken by faith! Although there are countless references to validate this truth, let's look at two more examples:

"But having the same spirit of faith, according to what is written, 'I believed, therefore I spoke,' we also believe, therefore also we speak." (2 Corinthians 4:13) Speaking is what releases the creative force of faith. That's why Jesus said we are going to have what we say. What you get may not be what you desire, so I suggest you get your tongue and your desires in agreement.

"But what does it say? 'The word is near you, in your mouth and in your heart' – that is, the word of faith which we are preaching." (Romans 10:8). When you put the word in your mouth, it gets into your heart. When it gets into your heart, it gets back it into your mouth and is released to give substance to what you expect to receive from the Lord. Just as simple as sowing seed!

SHE ACTED. The Bible is full of accounts in which men and women acted on their faith. Unlike many who just sit around and wait for God to drop the blessings on them. Those people never receive. They just gripe and complain about why God healed so and so, but for some reason he doesn't want to heal them. I want to tell you about a woman who didn't know the words "give up."

"And behold, a Canaanite woman came out from that region, and began to cry out, saying, "Have mercy on me, O Lord, Son of David; my daughter is cruelly demon possessed." But He did not answer her a word. And His disciples came to Him and kept asking Him, saying, "Send her away, for she is shouting out after us." But He answered and said, "I was sent only to the lost sheep of the house of Israel." But she came and began to bow down before Him, saying, "Lord, help me!" And He answered and said, "It is not good to take the children's bread and throw it to the dogs." But she said, "Yes, Lord; but even the dogs feed on the crumbs which fall from their masters table." Then Jesus answered and said to her, "O woman, your faith is great; be it done for you as you wish." And her daughter was healed at once." (Matthew 15:22-28)

This woman began to cry out after Jesus on behalf of her demon possessed daughter. Jesus did not answer her with a word. Why not? Because there would have been enough faith in that word to deliver her daughter. The next statement from Jesus seems strange:

"It is not good to take the children's bread and throw it to the dogs." You see, the Gentiles did not have a covenant with God. They were considered as animals or dogs by the Jewish people. However, we know that a dog has a soul, but not a spirit. We know they have emotions, and emotions are part of the soul. The response of the woman amazed Jesus. She said, "Yes, Lord, but even dogs eat the crumbs which fall from their master's table." This woman would not quit! She realized that even the crumbs will cause you to be healed! Jesus was sent only to the lost sheep of the house of Israel. But this woman was able to tap into the healing provision that wasn't even available to her. The Lord can never deny faith. She came to Him with great faith and left with desire fulfilled. Praise God!

One of the greatest accounts of acting on faith for healing is found in Acts 14:8–10: *"And at Lystra there was sitting a certain man, without strength in his feet, lame from his mother's womb, who had never walked. This man was listening to Paul as he spoke, who, when he had fixed his gaze upon him, and had seen that he had faith to be made well, said with a loud voice, "Stand upright on your feet." And he leaped up and began to walk."*

The Apostle Paul, on a missionary journey, was teaching people who are not Bible College graduates, highly educated, or familiar with the teaching of faith. A man lame from birth listening as Paul preached, and Paul perceived by the gift of the "Word of Knowledge" that the lame man had faith to be made whole.

We must ask ourselves two questions: 1) Where did this lame man get faith to be made whole? 2) If he had faith to be made whole, why was he still lame? The lame man received the faith to be healed by hearing the Word that Paul preached. It doesn't say what Paul preached, but he must have been teaching about healing because healing faith comes from the Word that promises healing. And we know that *"Faith comes by hearing and hearing by the Word of God."* (Romans 10:17) The reason the man was still lame, even though he had faith to be made whole, was because he had not yet acted on his faith. Paul gave him an opportunity when he commanded the man to stand upright on his feet. Faith demanded the lame man do what his mind, circumstance, and his own feet declared that he could not do. When he acted on his faith, he was healed. If the man from Lystra could receive faith by hearing the Word, act on it, and rise up healed, so can you.

SHE RECEIVED. The woman who had the issue of blood was made whole only after she obtained hope, received faith by hearing, and acted on that faith. So many people want to see and feel it first before they believe. But that's opposite to the way the kingdom of God works. God gave us our five senses that we might identify with this physical realm. But he gave us faith to identify with the spirit world in which we live. You cannot use your sensory perception to receive his promised provisions. You must first believe and then you will receive. You did not see Jesus before you believed in him. You believed without seeing him. Healing works the same way. You believe on the inside before it comes and manifests itself on the outside.

A doctor tells a woman that she is pregnant. There is no evidence of a child at this stage. She takes the doctor at his word. As time progresses, she begins to see proof of her conception. When God's promises of healing get into your heart, a conception takes place. You are pregnant, in a sense, with a promise. That promise of healing grows within you until one day you give birth to it. You had it before everyone else saw it; it was conceived by faith!

We spent time discussing Mark 11:22–23 concerning having

the God kind of faith and moving mountains by having what you say. Now, I want us to look at verse twenty-four of Mark, Chapter 11: *"Therefore I say unto you, what things soever ye desire, when ye pray, believe that ye receive them, and ye shall have them."* Notice that Jesus stated concerning the things you desire, when you pray, believe that you receive them. What are you to believe? The things you desire. When are you to believe that you receive the things you desire? When you get them? No! When you pray. What will you receive? That which you believe.

There are people who desire things from God, but what they desire and what they pray are sometimes two different things. Pray what you desire and believe you receive what you desire the moment you pray, then rejoice. If you rejoice when you get the manifestation of your desire, you are stating that you did not believe you received when you prayed. You stumbled into your desire somehow. After you believe what you receive when you pray, never ask for that desire or request again. If you do, you are saying you didn't believe that you received the first time you prayed. After you pray the initial time, from then on thank God for the thing you believe to you received when you prayed. Pray, believe, receive, and rejoice! Now go back and meditate on what we just discussed about Mark 11:24. You didn't get it all the first time. If you pray in faith for something more than once, you have dug up your seed. A seed can't sprout and develop if you keep digging it up!

Now let's finish the story about the woman with the issue of blood: *"And Jesus, immediately knowing in himself that virtue had gone out of him, turned him about in the press, and said, "Who touched my clothes?" And his disciples said on him, "Thou seest the multitude thronging thee, and sayest thou, who touched me?" And he looked roundabout to see her that had done this thing. But the woman fearing and trembling, knowing what was done in her, came and fell down before him, and told him all the truth. And he said unto her, "Daughter, thy faith hath made thee whole; go in peace, and be whole of thy plague."* (Mark 5:30-34)

Jesus felt power leave Him and asked the disciples, "who touched me?" They responded, "Jesus, everybody is touching you!" But Jesus knew that someone had touched him with faith. No doubt some people touched him to see if something would happen. It didn't. Some people touched him to see if perhaps sparks would fly out from Him; there were none. This woman believed that when she touched the tassel on the hem of His garment, she would be healed, and she was.

Numbers 15:38–40 teaches us about the tassel on Jesus's garment: *"Speak to the sons of Israel and tell them that they shall make for themselves tassels on the corners of their garments throughout their generations, and that they shall put on the tassel of each corner a cord of blue. And it shall be a tassel for you to look at and remember all the commandments of the Lord, so as to do them and not follow after your own heart and your own eyes, after which you played the harlot, in order that you may remember to do all My commandments and be holy to your God."*

This woman was touching a type of the Word. Jesus is the Word personified. You may say, "Well, if Jesus were here, I would be healed." Not necessarily. We must understand that the multitude thronging Jesus didn't receive anything. Although Jesus is not here now in physical manifestation, His word is. 1 Peter 2:24 says it best: *"And He Himself bore our sins in His body on the cross, that we might die to sin and live to righteousness; for by His stripes, you were healed." Did you notice that we WERE healed?* This uneducated woman did four simple things that caused her to

43

tap into the healing power of God: she heard, she said, she acted, and she received!

The final thing that I want to point out about this story is the very last thing Jesus said to the woman, "Daughter, thy faith hath made thee whole." Notice He did not say it was His faith that made her whole. Jesus stated that her faith had everything to do with her being healed. This is good news for us because, if her faith made her whole, then your faith can make you whole.

CHAPTER SEVEN

THE AUTHORITY OF THE BELIEVER

There are two banners under which Christians abide in the body of Christ. The first is the banner of the sovereignty of God. Here, it is believed that God is in absolute control. Everything that happens is preordained by him to fulfill all his plans and purposes. If sickness comes, then God must be trying to teach us something. I was listening to a radio preacher a while back as I was driving to the church one morning. His opening statement was: "I hope you were in the house of God yesterday, unless you were providently hindered." I said out loud in the car, "Providently hindered! Is this the new politically correct term for Gad keeping believers from church?

Let's examine this outburst of religious ignorance in the light of the Word. In Hebrews 10:25, we read, ***"not forsaking our own assembling together, as is the habit of some, but encouraging one another and all the more, as you see the day drawing near."*** So, let's get this straight. It is God's will for us to be present when the saints assemble together. But at the same time, God, out of His Divine providence, hinders us by making us sick or causing some tragedy in our lives so that we cannot assemble with the saints. Would it not be logical to conclude that God is working against His own purpose? That's ignorance personified in the form of a radio preacher! If that's the case, we need to be praying for God, since He cannot make up His mind whether or not He wants us in church!

Why is it some people in the body of Christ cast their common sense to the wind after their saved? James 1:17 gives us the true nature and character of God: ***"Every good thing bestowed, and every perfect gift is from above, coming down from the Father of lights, with whom there is no variation, or shifting shadow."*** Those under this banner of sovereignty believe that you must pray "if it is His will" concerning sickness and disease. The only time "if" should be included in prayer is when the will of God is not known. As in the prayer of dedicating yourself to the plan of God for your life because you can't find chapter and verse for that.

Again, let's find out what the Word of God says concerning the will of God: ***"And this is the confidence that we have in Him, that if we ask anything according to His will, He hears us. And if we know that He hears us in whatever we ask, we know that we have the requests which we have asked from Him."*** (1 John 5:14-15). Notice the term "confidence". You cannot have confidence and uncertainty at the same time. "But Pastor Brad," you may ask, "doesn't it say to ask according to His will? Yes, it does, but we must know what His will is in order to ask with confidence.

Let me enlighten you with a couple of scripture references:

- ***"So, then do not be foolish, but understand what the will of the Lord is."*** (Ephesians 5:17) Does this not look as if we are to know what His will is?
- ***"And he said, the God of our fathers has appointed you to know His will, and to see the Righteous One, and to hear an utterance from His mouth."*** (Acts 22:14) The Apostle Paul stated it is appointed onto us to know what His will is. Christians make religious statements, such as, "You just never know about God," or "God works in mysterious ways." I admit that in the Old Testament, God was somewhat of a mystery to people in that they didn't know Him. But in the New Covenant, He has revealed

Himself to us as never before.

- Again, let's see what the Apostle Paul says about the will of God: *"he made known to us the mystery of his will, according to his kind intention which he purposed in him."* (Ephesians 1:9)

I submit to you that the will of God is the Word of God. Your bible translation even states that it is the last WILL and testament of Jesus Christ. So, lets read 1 John 5:14 this way: *"And this is the confidence which we have before Him, that, if we ask anything according to His WORD, He hears us. And if we know that He hears us in whatever we ask, we know that we have the requests which we have asked from Him."* If we ask according to the Word, we have confident access before Him and He hears us. Seeing that He hears us, we know that we have our request answered! To the people who say, "You just never know about God," I say, "Read the Bible!"

The second banner under which believers rally is called the authority of the believer. To understand authority, we must go to the book of Genesis. In chapter one, versus twenty-six through twenty-eight, we find the creation of man and the authority delegated to him:

"Then God said, "Let us make man in Our image, according to Our likeness; and let them rule over the fish of the sea and over the birds of the sky and over the cattle and over all the earth, and over every creeping thing that creeps upon the earth." And God created man in His own image, in the image of God He created him; male and female He created them. And God blessed them; and God said unto them, "be fruitful, multiply, and fill the earth, and subdue it; and rule over the fish of the sea and over the birds of the sky, and over every living thing that moves on the earth."

Adam is made in the image and likeness of God. Like God, Adam was made to rule over everything on this planet: everything that flew in the air, swam in the waters, and moved on the surface of the earth. The way Adam was to utilize his authority was the same way God had when He recreated the earth: with faith-filled words. Adam was commissioned by God to be the God of this world.

Chapter three of Genesis reveals the Adam and Eve ate from the tree of the knowledge of good and evil. In doing so, Adam bowed his knee to that outlaw spirit called Satan and died spiritually. Now, the earth became subleased to God's enemy, and sin entered the world. Sin gave birth to sickness, poverty, and death. 2 Corinthians 4:4 reveals Satan's position concerning the lease: ***"In whose case the god of this world has blinded the minds of the unbelieving, that they might not see the light of the gospel of the glory of Christ, who is the image of God."***

When God called Adam and Eve to accountability, he prophesied that through the seed of the woman the head of the enemy would be bruised. two thousand years later, God entered into a blood covenant with a man called Abram. He gave him a promise that he would be the father of nations, and through his seed all the earth would be blessed. For twenty-four years, Abram was not any closer to the promise of a child than the day God gave it. So, God changed Abram's name to Abraham, which means, "father of nations." In doing so, God forced him to call for what he didn't have, and in less than a year he had the promised child. When Isaac had grown into a young man, God told Abraham to go to the mountain that he would show him and there offer Isaac as a sacrifice. Why would God do such a thing? In order for God to offer his son, Abraham had to be willing to offer his son. Let's look at the reference:

"And Abraham took the wood of the burnt offering and laid

48

it upon Isaac his son; and he took the fire in his hand, and a knife; and they went both of them together. And Isaac spoke unto Abraham his father, and said, my father: and he said, Here am I, my son. And he said, behold the fire and the wood: but where is the lamb for a burnt offering? And Abraham said, my son, God will provide Himself a lamb for a burnt offering: so, they went both of them together. And they came to the place which God had told him of; and Abraham built an altar there, and laid the wood in order, and bound Isaac his son, and laid him on the altar upon the wood. And Abraham stretched forth his hand and took the knife to slay his son. And the angel of the Lord called unto him out of heaven, and said, Abraham, Abraham: and he said, here am I. And he said, lay not thine hand upon the lad, neither do thou anything unto him: for now, I know that thou fearest God, seeing thou hast not withheld thy son, thine only son from me. And Abraham lifted up his eyes, and looked, and behold behind him a ram caught in a thicket by his horns: and Abraham went and took the ram and offered him up for a burnt offering in the stead of his son. And Abraham called the name of that place Jehovah Jireh: as it is said to this day, In the mount of the Lord it shall be seen. And the angel of the Lord called unto Abraham out of heaven the second time, And said, by myself have I sworn, saith the Lord, for because thou hast done this thing, and hast not withheld thy son, thine only son: that in blessing I will bless thee, and in multiplying I will multiply thy seed as the stars of the heaven, and as the sand which is upon the sea shore; and thy seed shall possess the gate of his enemies" (Genesis 22:6-17)

When God saw that Abraham was willing to offer his son, He considered that he had done it (offered Isaac), and it was then legal for God to send His Son as a sacrifice. Two thousand years later, like Isaac, Jesus walked up the same hill carrying the wood for His sacrifice. Isaac was the fulfillment of the promise God made

49

to Abraham that he would be the father of Nations. Jesus was the fulfillment of the seed of Abraham that would bruise the serpent's head and redeem mankind.

Our flesh gives us legal authority in the earth. When we die, the only thing that gives us access to the earth is a will. Jesus is no longer here in His physical body, but His will (which is His Word) is, and His will is in force so long as God can find those who will offer their bodies of flesh to establish His will on planet Earth.

Let me explain how both Jesus and Satan gained entrance into the earth:

"Truly, truly I say to you, he who does not enter by the door into the fold of the sheep, but climbs up some other way, he is a thief and a robber. But he who enters by the door is a shepherd of the sheep. To him the doorkeeper opens; and the sheep hear his voice, and he calls his own sheep by name, and leads them out." (John 10:1-3)

The door represents Jesus' legal entry into the earth. Redemption had to come by a man. Man sinned; therefore, man had to redeem himself. Sadly, all mankind was tainted with sin and there was not one whose blood was pure enough to pay the ransom of Adam's treason. So, Jesus laid aside His Godhead powers, humbled Himself, took upon Himself a robe of flesh that gave Him the authority to live His life without sin and die in our place.

Satan was once an angel of God called Lucifer who led a coup against God and was thrown out of heaven along with the angels who followed him. Satan devised a plan to get back at God by taking over God's prized creation: mankind, who was created in the image and likeness of God. Understand that Satan is the illegal one who "climbed up another way" by borrowing the body of a serpent. This was the only way that Satan could legally bring temptation into the earth. I said all of this so you can see the fact that your body of flesh gives you authority in the earth! This is why Satan wants to destroy your body with sickness and disease. As long as you live on this planet, you are a potential threat to him and his kingdom of darkness. The reason Satan fights so hard against the faith message is because once you couple the right to rule and reign with the creative force of faith, Satan's days of dominating you are over!

Let's look at this authority in operation with the disciples of Jesus: *"And he called the twelve together and gave them power and authority over all the demons, and to heal diseases. And he sent them out to proclaim the kingdom of God, and to perform healing."* (Luke 9:1-2) Jesus sent His disciples out with power and authority to cast out demons and to perform healing. They needed power because authority is the right to use power. Jesus got this power when John baptized Him, and the Holy Spirit came upon Him to empower Him to do the works of God and destroy the works of the devil. This is the same power we find today through the baptism of the Holy Spirit that Jesus spoke of in Acts, chapter eight: *"But you shall receive power when the Holy Spirit has come upon you; and you shall be My witness both in Jerusalem, and in all Judea and Samaria, and even to the remotest part of the earth."*

In Luke, chapter ten, Jesus sent out seventy disciples as He had the twelve. Notice what they said upon their return:

"And the seventy returned with joy, saying, "Lord, even the demons are subject to us in Your name." And He said to them, "I was watching Satan fall from the heavens like lightning. Behold,

I have given you authority to tread upon serpents and scorpions, and over all the power of the enemy, and nothing shall hurt you."

Jesus said He beheld Satan falling like lightning and losing his grip on humanity as the disciples healed the sick and cast out demons. Jesus also stated that authority to tread upon the enemy and his power has been given to us. Praise God!

CHAPTER EIGHT

THE NAME OF JESUS

And there is salvation in no one else; for there is no other name under heaven that has been given among men, by which we must be saved." (Acts 4:12). The name of Jesus is above every name and has been given to the body of Christ. This means we have power and attorney, written legal authority, to use His name and to conduct his affairs on the earth until His return.

I have been to Kenya, Africa many times. Once I was there for about three weeks to conduct several open-air crusades. Before I left, I signed a power of attorney over to my wife, in order to carry out my affairs until I returned. This meant that she could sign my name to any document, legally binding me to any covenant without me even being there. Think about the authority this represents! She could have sold our house or bought a new car in my absence. So just think about the business that we can do for the kingdom of God by having the right to use the name of Jesus. We can cast out demons, heal the sick, set the captives free, obtain promises, and reap the harvest of humanity before Jesus returns.

The Apostle Peter, who never seemed to be able to "get it together" until he was endued with power at Pentecost, was going with John to the temple at the hour of prayer. Let's see how this power of attorney worked in his life:

"And a certain man who had been lame from his mother's womb was being carried along, whom they used to sit down every day at the gate of the temple, which is called Beautiful, in order

to beg alms of those who were entering the temple. And when he saw Peter and John about to go into the temple, he began asking to receive alms. And Peter, along with John, fixed his gaze upon him and said, "look at us!" And he began to give them his attention, expecting to receive something from them. But Peter said, "I do not possess silver and gold, but what I do have I give to you: in the name of Jesus Christ of Nazarene – walk!" And seizing him by the right hand, he raised him up; and immediately his feet and his ankles were strengthened. And with a leap, he stood upright and began to walk; and he entered the temple with them, walking and leaping and praising God. And all the people who saw him walking and praising God." (Acts 3:2-9)

The lame man was expecting to receive something. Peter had "the something" that he needed. What was it? It was the name of Jesus! Verse sixteen of Acts, chapter 3, sheds light on how this healing took place: *"and on the basis of faith in his name, it is the name of Jesus which has strengthened this man whom you see and know; and the faith which comes through Him has given him this perfect health in the presence of you all."* Faith in the name of Jesus healed the man, "the faith which comes through Him".

This is consistent with Romans 10:17, which reads, *"Faith comes by hearing, and hearing by the Word of God."* John 1:1 says, *"In the beginning was the Word, and the Word was with God, and the Word was God."* You see, Jesus is the Word personified. Jesus and the Word are one.

I want to show you another example of what faith in the name of Jesus can accomplish:

"And it happened that as we were going to the place of prayer, a certain slave-girl having a spirit of divination met us, who was

bringing her masters much profit by fortunetelling. Following after Paul and us, she kept crying out, saying, "These men are bondservants of the most high God, who are proclaiming to you the way of salvation." And she continued doing this for many days. But Paul was greatly annoyed, and turned and said to the spirit, "I command you in the name of Jesus Christ to come out of her!" And it came out at that very moment. But when her masters saw that their hope of profit was gone, they seized Paul and Silas and dragged them into the marketplace before the authorities." (Acts 16:16-19)

What this demon said was true. Paul and Silas were men of God showing the way of salvation. First, notice the demon didn't say "showing us the way." There's no redemption for evil spirits. Second, who wants a demon witnessing for you? I believe this was said in a mocking manner. But when Paul became greatly annoyed at what the demon was doing, he commanded it to come out in the name of Jesus, and it came out! Legally speaking, all things have been placed under the feet of Jesus. But we must appropriate what Jesus bought and paid for with his own shed blood.

Let's look at what Ephesians 1:19-23 says:

"And what is the surpassing greatness of His power toward us who believe. These are in accordance with the working of the strengths of His might which He brought about in Christ, when He raised Him from the dead, and seated Him at His right hand in the heavenly places, far above all rule and authority and power and dominion, and every name that is named, not only in this age, but also in the one to come. And He put all things in subjection under His feet and gave Him as head over all things to the church, which is His body, the fullness of Him who fills all in all."

First, notice that resurrection power is available to us who believe. Second, the name of Jesus is above all other names and powers. Third, all things are under His feet. You might be thinking, "Well, but that's Jesus and His feet are in heaven." Notice that it said Jesus is the head and we are the body. The feet are not a part of the head; they are a part of the body, and we are parts of the many membered body of Christ. So, since we are the body and the feet are in the body, then all things have been placed under our feet praise God! Fourth, since sickness has a name, then the name of Jesus is above it and it is under our feet. When you become fed up with sickness, disease, poverty, and defeat, the name of Jesus is available for use at any time.

CHAPTER NINE

COUNTER ATTACKS

I have seen many individuals obtain healing through faith, and then lose their healing through what I call a counterattack. For you to fully understand how Satan counters what you receive from God, let's first look at how healing comes to us.

There are various methods to administer healing, but only two basic ways to receive it from God:

1) One way is by the gifts of the spirit found in 1 Corinthians, chapter twelve. Understand these gifts operate as the Holy Spirit wills. These gifts usually occur when a person is ministering under the anointing of "gifts of healing" or the "working of miracles." You cannot make the gifts operate when you will, but rather when He wills.

2) The other way to receive healing is through faith, by taking a stand on the Word of God. This is the highest form of receiving. Because if you get it by the Word rather than a spiritual gift, you will not be subject to losing it through a counterattack.

Satan is a thief; he takes pleasure in robbing you from your inheritance. Such is also the nature of demons or unclean spirits. There's an account found in Matthew 12:43–45:

"Now when the unclean spirit goes out of a man, it passes through waterless places, seeking rest, and does not find it, then it says, "I will return to my house from which I came;" and when

it comes, it finds it unoccupied, swept, and put an order. Then it goes and takes along with it seven other spirits more wicked than itself, and they go in and live there; and the last state of that man becomes worse than the first. That is the way it will also be with the evil generation."

I want you to notice in this reference that the kingdom of darkness is structured to counter anything that it sees as a threat. Satan doesn't care whether you go to heaven or hell. In either place you are out of his hair, so to speak. The only place you are a threat to him is here on planet earth. But only if you realize who you are in and of Christ Jesus and utilize the authority delegated in the name of Jesus.

The apostle Paul taught about the armor of God in Ephesians chapter six. He said in verse sixteen: *"Above all, taking the shield of faith, wherewith ye shall be able to quench all the fiery darts of the wicked one."* When you are standing in faith, you hold a shield that will quench not some of, but all the fiery darts or attacks of the enemy. Once you are in faith, there is nothing he can do to stop you. His only strategy is to counter your position with doubt, or what I call a lying symptom of the suffering from which you were healed. That's when you must resist him firmly in faith. James 4:7 tells us to *"submit therefore to God. Resist the devil and he will flee from you."*

A better scheme for the kingdom of darkness is to keep you from the Word of God to begin with. Because if he can keep you from the truth of the Word, then you cannot have faith since faith comes from the Word. I want to prove this point in the Scriptures: *"The Sower sows the word. And these are the ones who are beside the road where the Word is sown; and when they hear, immediately Satan comes and takes away the Word which has been sown in them.* " (Mark 4:14-15) If we look at these verses, it seems to say that Satan is going to steal the word from us, and there's nothing we can do about it.

However, if we compare Matthew's account of the same parable, we see he added something that Mark did not add: *"When anyone hears the Word of the kingdom, and does not understand it, the evil one comes and snatches away what has been sown in his heart. This is the one on whom seed was sown beside the road."* (Matthew 13:19) Matthew wrote that anyone who hears the Word and does not UNDERSTAND it will have it taken away by the evil one. Please realize that Satan gets everything you do not understand, but he gets nothing that you do understand!

And 1994, I preached a crusade in the city of Kericho, Kenya. A girl who was twelve years old came up in the line where I was laying hands on the sick. I could see that she had suffered from polio sometime earlier and had no use of her left arm. When I laid hands on her, immediately her arm was healed, and she testified on the platform that God had healed her.

Two nights later, as I was again ministering to the sick, I saw her in the healing line. At first, I wondered what she was doing there; perhaps something else was wrong with her. By the time she got up to me, I knew by a "word of knowledge" that she had lost her healing. You see, the devil launched a counterattack and caused her to doubt her healing. I said to her, "well, I see that you have lost your healing." She replied, "yes, but if you will lay hands on me again, I'll be healed and never doubt it again." I laid my hands on her and again her arm was completely healed. Praise the Lord!

I don't want you to get the wrong impression. Not everyone to whom I have taught these principles to over the past forty some years were healed. One of them is someone I dearly loved. A precious young lady, who became a "daughter in the Lord" to me was healed of cancer throughout her entire body. It was an astonishing testimony of God's healing power! Later, she had a counterattack in a different area of her body and died as a result of it. I tried my best to get her to fight the good fight of faith again, but she gave up. Burying her was one of the hardest things I have ever done. From that great loss, I learned the value of emphasizing the fact that Satan will stop at nothing to discredit God's Word.

After healing comes to you, be prepared for the enemy's counterattack. When it comes, rise up in faith and say, "No thank you. I am healed and I deny sickness the right to exist in my body!"

CHAPTER TEN

THE LIFESTYLE OF FAITH

Faith is a lifestyle – not magic. The problem with most people is they pass on the daily opportunities to act in faith. They wait until they have a mountain in their life before they think to consider God's healing provision. Again, I have no problem with the medical profession; but if you always run to the doctor and never utilize the Word of God, you may not have time to develop yourself in faith. I want to share a true story with you that happened a few years ago in my life and you will see the importance of living by faith and being prepared for whatever may come against you. One morning I woke and quickly realized that I was very sick and sensed that I was dying. I was rushed to the doctor who after examining me and finding an extremely high white blood count sent me to the hospital. The surgeon stated that I needed immediate abdominal surgery and that he might have to remove my intestines and other organs necessary. I knew then, I was either where I needed to be in faith, or I wasn't. There would be no time to gather more faith for healing at that moment. When I awoke from the surgery, the doctor was there and stated that I had had three miracles take place. You don't hear doctors throwing around the term "miracles" very often! The first miracle he said was that my appendix had ruptured four months earlier and I should have died after forty-eight hours or so. Second, my appendix was healing itself and the appendix doesn't normally do so and by observing the state of skin regrowth, he could tell when it had ruptured. Third, my body was getting rid of the toxic waste, but some had gotten onto my intestines and twisted a section shut and that was the reason I almost died. He said if that had not happened, then I would have never known that my appendix had ruptured. An MRI had been taken and a fourth miracle was discovered: a spleen that I had lost in a motorcycle accident back in 1981 had grown back! Thank God that the lifestyle of faith I have lived was enough to bring forth the miraculous even when my own body had become a weapon formed against me. Had I waited until the attack to get faith from the Word of God, I would not be alive today. I believe in pre-maintenance where faith is concerned. Often, I declare that healing power flows through my body and that no weapon formed against me can prosper. As I have said before, the Word of God works when you work it, but it won't if you don't.

While in Bible College in 1980 I realized that I could receive healing if I got sick, but it would be better to live a life of health. I declared that I would live free from sickness and disease. Not long after my declaration I got sick with the flu. After three days I had become well again. I was disappointed and a little upset that faith hadn't worked. Later that day the Lord asked me what my problem was. I told him that the Word didn't work. "Oh, so it doesn't work," the Lord responded? I told him, "No" as I had believed to be healed and that it had taken three days to recover. He then asked me if I knew anyone else who had been sick with the flu. I mentioned several others that I knew who had the flu. "How long did they have the flu the Lord asked." I stated they had had the flu a week to ten days. That's when the revelation hit me: it did work! I had been healed in three days rather than a week or more! I then said out loud: "If I can get rid of the flu in three days, I can get rid of it in two days. If I can get rid of it in two days, I can get rid of it in one day. If I can get rid of it in one day, I can get rid of it when the symptoms touch my body!" That day began my journey to walking in health. I didn't develop myself in a day, week or even months. It took time to learn how to appropriate the promises of health and healing that Father God has made available by the shed blood of Jesus. If you have a mountain of sickness in your life, now is the time to begin to declare the Word of God's healing provision. If you are healthy, now is the time to act on the Word with the small attacks and begin walking in health by living the lifestyle faith.

CHAPTER ELEVEN

THINGS YOU SHOULD DO

LIVE TO RIGHTEOUSNESS - I want to help you with what you should do after you have believed to receive your healing. We have been trained to be works oriented. But we need to understand that we are the righteousness of God. Jesus didn't just take on sin, but rather became sin for us, He became sin that we might be made the righteousness of God in Him: *"He made Him who knew no sin to be sin on our behalf, that we might become the righteousness of God in Him."* (2 Corinthians 5:21)

One of the greatest teachings we need to understand is the revelation of righteousness. Most people are law oriented and attempt to receive healing through works rather than realizing healing is a gift. Jesus did the redemptive work so we can freely receive that which He paid for by becoming sin for us and providing healing by the wounds on His back: *"and He Himself bore our sins in His body on the cross, that we might die to sin and live to righteousness; for by His strips you were healed."* (1 Peter 2:24) because we are the righteousness of God healing belongs to us. Stop trying to work for healing - and simply let healing work for you. Often, I have observed people that I have laid hands on become chatty with prayer trying to "do" something to earn the healing they so desire. It is because they feel unworthy, and they think they have to work for it. If you understand who you are in Him, you will realize that you are worthy in Christ and healing is not based on personal merit. You ARE the righteousness of God!

STOP BELIEVING – What I mean by this is you must believe and then stop "believing." As long as you are in the "believing mode" you are still in the process. Often, I hear Christians state that they are "believing" God for their healing. The problem with their confession is they have not come to the end of their faith. The Bible states in 2 Corinthians 4:3–14 *"but having the same spirit of faith, according to what is written, "I believed; therefore, I spoke," we also believe, therefore also we speak."* Believe once, rest, and then start thanking and praising God for what you have believed to receive.

ENTER INTO REST – Once you have believed to receive you healing it's time to enter into rest. I imagine that most of you have ordered a product on the internet or at least understand how the process works. You find the product that is available to you and take ownership of it by filling out the information and paying for it with perhaps your MasterCard. Once you hit the enter button it is now yours. You may get an email describing the details but, for the most part, you don't have to do anything else but rest and wait patiently for your product to arrive. You will most likely tell others what you now have, even though you still can't see it. Wow, you did all that in total faith - you believed to receive something you could not see or feel and thought nothing of it. The transaction was a total step of faith and you rested until it arrived. Why should the promises of God be any different? Realize that the internet is a physical representation of what Father God has had all along to bridge the gap between the spiritual and physical realm.

CHAPTER TWELVE

QUESTIONS & ANSWERS

1. The doctor says I need an operation. Should I let him operate? If you have to ask the question, then by all means have the operation. Why? Because you may not have enough time to develop yourself in faith. Believe God on the level you are on and then get beyond that by walking in faith. I want to make it clear as I have stated many times that I am not against the medical profession. I understand, however, that doctors are not healers. They aide the natural healing of the body. They may have to put something in or take something out. God created the human body, and he knows how to repair it. The problem with always running to the doctor and not developing your faith is this: What if you have a problem and the doctor says there's nothing he can do to help? Well, you either believe God or you die.

2. Since I have trusted God for my healing, should I continue to take my medication? By all means. If a doctor put you on medication and you agreed to take it, let the doctor take you off it. Realize that you BELIEVE that you are healed, but you may not be healed as a manifested fact. When the healing is evident, it will be evident to everyone including your doctor, who will then realize the medication is no longer needed. I know a man who believed for the healing of his eyes so that he would no longer need glasses. He continued to wear his glasses until he could no longer see with them on. Besides if you have a restriction on your driver's license that requires you to wear corrective lenses, then it would be against the law not to do so. Plus, you'll be doing the rest of us a favor!

3. I have been diagnosed with a terminal disease and given about six months to live. Should I continue medical treatment? I wouldn't if I were you. The reason I say this is because you have only a short time in which to develop yourself in faith. I find that continuing treatment in a "no-hope situation medically speaking is more of a hinderance to your faith rather than a help. I know this seems irrational, but I've seen too many people put their confidence in the medical profession in a no-win situation, and at the last-minute attempt to trust the Word. The sad part is that there is not enough time left to unlearn some old things whiling learning some new things.

4. Can I pray that God will give me more faith? No, you cannot. Faith comes by hearing, and hearing by the Word of God. The more of God's Word that you have abiding in you, the more faith you have. Your ability to ask in faith depends on the Word level in your life. For instance, John 15:7 teaches that once the words of God abide within you, you can ask what you will: *"If you abide in Me, and My words abide in you, ask whatever you will, and it shall be done for you."* Here, Jesus is saying that if we abide in Him, or if we are born again, and His Words, which have faith in them, abide in us, then the creative force of faith will cause what we desire to come to pass.

5. If God wants everyone healed, why doesn't He empty the hospitals? This is a common perception among people who do not understand the operation of God's kingdom and the free moral agency of mankind. First, not everyone who is sick desires to be healed by faith. Second, for God to heal everyone in the hospitals, He would be violating the freedom of choice that He has given to them. If He were to do that, then why not just go ahead and save all people without their believing in Him? Third, God is not need minded. If God were need minded, there would be no needs today in the earth. During the ministry of Jesus, there were multitudes who weren't healed. Who not? The Bible states in Luke 5:15, *"But the news about Him was spreading even farther, and great multitudes were gathering to hear Him and to be healed of their sickness."* Notice that they came to be healed. Jesus did not search out those who were sick. The soil is not need minded. The soil proclaims, "give me some seed, and I will give you a harvest." Jesus said the kingdom of God is like sowing seed. In Mark 4:26-28 we have this account: *"And He was saying, 'The kingdom of God is like a man who casts seed upon the soil; and goes to bed at night and gets up by day, and the seed sprouts up and grows - - how, he himself does not know. The soil produces crops by itself; first the blade, then the head, then the mature grain in the head."* The seed places a demand on the soil just as the healing seed of God's Word places a demand on God's healing provision.

6. If we walk in divine health, then how are we going to die? This is a good question; the answer is, by faith. *"For in it the righteousness of God is revealed from faith to faith; as it is written, But the righteous man shall live by faith."* (Romans 1:17) Not only should we live by faith, but we should also die by faith. Many of the patriarchs of old knew when they were going to die. Israel gathered his sons and grandsons around his bed. He blessed them and prophesied to them and then gathered his feet into his bed and died by faith. It is appointed unto man to die but not until we have fulfilled the number of our days. Psalm 91:15-16 sheds light on this subject: *"He will call upon me, and I will answer him; I will be with him in troubles; I will rescue him and honor him. With a long life I will satisfy him and let him behold My salvation."* Isn't it amazing that when people are sick, they say they want to die, but when they are healed, they say they want to live? God placed the desire to live - - and to live satisfied - - on the inside of us.

7. Isn't faith just bossing God around? The critics of the faith message think that's what we are doing, but nothing could be further from the truth. Faith is not placing a demand on God. Instead, it is placing a demand on something He wants us to have: His healing provision obtained by the blood of His Son Jesus. Let me ask you a question: Are you placing a demand on God when you name and claim salvation? No, you are placing a demand on something He wants you to have. In most circles, it is politically correct to confess and possess salvation but frowned upon when it comes to healing, victorious living, and financial prosperity.

8. What do I say when people ask me how I'm doing? I'll answer this first by saying what faith would not say. Faith would not say, "I don't hurt." It would not say, "I am healed for a physical fact," when the manifestation has not occurred. It would say however, that I may look sick, the doctor tells me I am sick, but I believe that healing power flows through me and perfects a healing and a cure within me and will not stop until I'm completely made whole. Remember this: Faith is not calling things that are, as though they were not; that is denial or Christian Science religion. Faith is Christian sense! Faith calls for what it doesn't have until it comes. The truth is that you were healed almost two thousand years ago and are just now receiving it. Matthew 8:17 says: ***"In order that what was spoken through Isaiah the prophet might be fulfilled, saying, 'He Himself took our infirmities, and carried away our diseases."*** First, notice that this is past tense. Since Jesus took our infirmities, then legally we no longer have them. Seeing that He carried away our diseases, those diseases are far from us. The word for *infirmities* in the Greek is "Asthenia." It means a minor ailment or condition, such as the common cold or a headache. The Greek word for *diseases* is "Nosos," which is a terminal condition, such as cancer or heary disease. When we put the meanings together, we understand that Jesus took everything from our minor conditions to our terminal conditions, everything from the common cold to HIV. Praise God forever! I've heard preachers say that Jesus was referring to spiritual healing. Well, it looks as if those same preachers would have had enough sense to look at the preceding verse and see that it is a physical healing to which the verse refers: *"And when evening had come, they brought to Him many who were demon-possessed; and He cast out the spirits with a word, and healed all who were ill."* (Matthew 8:16) Does this sound like spiritual healing to you? Preachers! They never cease to amaze me!

9. How long do I have to confess the Word concerning healing? Until you believe it. Notice that faith comes by hearing. Hearing who? Hearing you. Paul said in Romans 10:6-8: *"But the righteousness based on faith speaks thus, do not say in your heart, "Who will ascend into heaven?" (that is, to bring Christ down), or "Who will descend into the abyss?" (that is, to bring Christ up from the dead). But what does it say? The word is near you, in your mouth and in your heart (that is, the word of faith which we are preaching)."* Verses six and seven tell us that we don't need Jesus to come down from heaven in order for us to be healed. Neither does He have to be crucified again in order for us to obtain healing. But what does it say? The Word is near you. You put it in your mouth, and it gets in your heart. You speak the Word until you believe it. Jesus said in Mark 11:23 that you will have what you say so long as you believe and doubt not in your heart. When you first begin to declare that by His stripes you are healed, you most likely will not believe it. But keep saying it until you do believe it. Once you believe it, confession is not necessary. But if you are like me, I so love speaking the Word that I make confessions such as: "Father God, isn't it wonderful that I have already believed to receive. I thank you that Himself took my infirmities and carried away my diseases." I am no longer believing for healing, but rather thanking Him for it. Also, don't put God on a limitation of time. We get in trouble when we do that. God programmed us to believe what we say, but so many people today have fouled up that programming by constantly saying things that they don't desire. That's faith in reverse, or we could say fear. Fear is confidence in what you don't desire, while faith is confidence in what God said.

10. I still have thoughts about dying. What do I do? As long as you are in the earth, you will have thoughts that contradict the Word of God. But that Bible gives us the solution to these thoughts: *"For though we walk in flesh, we do not war according to the flesh, for the weapons of our warfare are not of the flesh, but mighty through God for the pulling down of strongholds. We are destroying speculations and every lofty thing raised up against the knowledge of God, and we are taking every thought captive to the obedience of Christ."* (2 Corinthians 10:3-5). Speculation and thoughts contrary to the Word are a form of temptation that will cause you to doubt. When Jesus was tempted by the devil, He responded by saying, "It is written." This is how we take thoughts captive to the obedience of Christ. I like what 1 Corinthians 10:13 says: *"No temptation has overtaken you, but such as is common to man; and God is faithful, who will not allow you to be tempted beyond what you are able, but with the temptation will provide the way of escape also, that you may be able to endure it."* First, the devil can only come against us with things that are common to us, such as tragedy, poverty, sickness, and defeat. Second, notice that you cannot be tempted beyond what you are able to overcome. So, the fact that the situation is exists states that you can overcome it, or it wouldn't be there! In a sense, God has the deck of life stacked in our favor. Third, God has provided us with the way of escape; it's called faith. The eleventh chapter of Hebrews is called the faith hall of fame. It is filled with examples of those who "by faith, conquered."

***11. If God wants everyone to be healed, then why did Aunt
Sarah die?*** Every church has an Aunt Sarah story. Here is the way
the story usually goes: "Aunt Sarah loved the Lord. She attended
church faithfully. Every time the church doors flew open, Aunt
Sarah flew in. If anybody had faith, it was old Aunt Sarah. She
stood up in the church and testified that she believed that one day
the Lord was going to heal her of cancer, and yet she died. See
there! It must not be God's will for everyone to be healed because
if it were, Aunt Sarah would have been healed." This question is
very easy to answer. It is a typical example of how people alter
the Word of God to fit their circumstance. To begin with, notice
that Aunt Sarah testified that she believed the Lord would heal
her one day. The truth is, by the stripes placed on the back of the
Lord Jesus Christ, she was already healed. Her healing was bought
and paid for nearly two thousand years ago. God has done all He
is going to do about healing just as He has done all He is going
to do about salvation. It's up to you and me to do what it takes to
receive that salvation readily available to us. People can testify
in church and say they believe they are healed, but when they get
around others, we find out what they really believe. What they
say to their spouse and Momma is what they really believe. This
causes confusion among the church members because the person
indicated that they were in faith. But perhaps they were writing
their will and making the funeral arrangements. Faith makes no
provision for failure. You and I don't know what Aunt Sarah really
believed until she was healed or died. Aunt Sarah didn't make a
faith connection. She didn't do what it took to receive her healing.
Most believers will admit that if a person does not accept Jesus as
Lord and Savior, that person will be cast into the lake of fire on
the Day of Judgement. We understand that they did not do what
it took to be saved. Yet, we are offended if someone such as me
comes along and says that Aunt Sarah died early in life because
she lacked the faith to receive healing. Why not declare that God

is unjust in sending people to the lake of fire because they only lacked the faith to be saved? Doesn't this appeal to the good sense that God blessed you with? As I stated in the introduction of this book, we all have a part to play. If you don't receive healing, it's your fault! It will not do you any good to be offended at me for stating the truth. The fact is that you can do what it takes to live a long life satisfied.

CHAPTER THIRTEEN

HEALING CONFESSIONS

These confessions have been made personal for your benefit. Romans 10:10 states the importance of confessing the Word of God: "… and with the mouth, confession is made unto salvation." This would also apply to whatever promise you are confessing. So, let's say it this way: confession is made unto healing! As we read earlier in proverbs 4:20–22, *"… my son, give attention to my words; incline your ear to my sayings. Do not let them depart from your site; keep them in the midst of your heart. For they are life to those who find them and medicine to all their flesh."* Just as a doctor might prescribed medicine for you and instruct you to take it three times a day until you are better, I want you to confess the scriptures three times a day until you believe what God has said about your healing:

Because I doubt not in my heart but believe those things that I say shall surely come to pass, I always have what I say. I can have what I say or say what I have. I choose to have what I say. (Mark 11:13)

Since life and death are in the power of my tongue, and I will surely eat the fruit of what I have said, I choose to speak words that carry faith and provide life. (Proverbs 18:21.)

As a wise man, I bring forth good things out of the good deposits of my heart, and out of the abundance of my heart, my mouth speaks. (Matthew 12:34–35)

I give voice to the Word of God, and the angels who are mighty in strength, obey, and perform the Word that I speak. (Psalm 103:20)

Just like the way the Father God operates, the words that proceeded out of my mouth do not return unto me void and empty but accomplish all my desire. (Isaiah 55:11)

Jesus took my, infirmities, so I don't have them. He carried away my diseases, so they are far from me. (Matthew 8:17)

The same spirit that raised Jesus from the dead dwells in me, and he that raised Jesus up also quickens and makes alive my mortal body by the spirit that dwells within me. (Romans 8:11)

Since the law of the spirit of life in Christ Jesus has set me free from the law of sin and death, I boldly say that every disease, germ, and virus that touches my body dies instantly in the name of Jesus. (Romans 8:2)

I bless the Lord with all my soul and do not forget his covenant benefits, he forgives all my iniquities, and heals all my diseases. (Psalm 103:2–3)

I always give attention to God's words; therefore, his words are life and medicine to all my flesh. Healing power flows through my body, perfecting a healing and a cure within me. (Proverbs 4:20–22)

Jesus bore my sins in his own body on the cross that I might die to sin and live for righteousness, and by his strips, I was healed. If I was, then I am. (1 Peter 2:24)

I buffet my body with the Word of God and make it my slave;

therefore, I never ask my body how it is feeling. I tell my body how it must feel and what it must do. (1 Corinthians 9:27)

I abide in the Lord Jesus Christ, and his words about in me, so I ask what I will, and it is done unto me. (John 15:7)

I speak the Word of God into my heart, and my spirit makes diligence search to cause the things which I desire to come to pass. (Psalm 77:6)

For this is the thing that keeps walking off the field of battle with the victory, even my faith. (1 John 5:4)

Jesus said, "…all things are possible to him that believes;" therefore, nothing is impossible for me because I believe. (Mark 9:23)

Above all things, I always take up the shield of faith and quench all the fiery darts of the wicked one. (Ephesians 6:16)

My faith gives substance to the things that I hope for. It is the evidence and title deed for the things I desire. (Hebrews 11:1)

CHAPTER FOURTEEN

HEARING AND DOING THE WORD

Critics of the faith message say that we teach the theory of never having any problems in life if we walk by faith. I've never taught that nor has anyone else that I know of. It never ceases to amaze me that ignorant people can hear one statement that you make and take it out of context. It's not that we don't have storms, such as sickness and disease; we just learn how to overcome them and walk in health.

Let me give you an example: several months ago, I went to a certain place of business to see a friend of mine. As I walked into the room, I noticed that my friend was talking to a man who I later learned was the pastor of a church not far away. As I approached them, I heard the pastor tell my friend that he usually makes three to four hospital visits per week. Once we had been in introduced, he asked me how many hospital visits I made per week. I said about three to four a year. He responded, "Three to four a year?! I must be preaching my people to death!" I just stood there thinking, "You most likely are." He then asked how many church members we had thinking our church must be smaller in size. Not so, we were larger. The pastor changed the subject after that. if I were that pastor, I would want to know what was being taught to the people at His Image Ministries so I could have the same results, but he didn't ask me. How sad! If you teach people how to receive healing and how to walk in divine health, you won't spend all your time making hospital visits! I want to close with one of the greatest teachings of Jesus. He summed up the sermon on the mount teaching by emphasizing two important ingredients needed for us to outlast the storms of life, and have good success:

"Therefore, everyone who hears these words of mine, and acts upon them, may be compared to a wise man, who built his house upon the rock. And the rain descended, and the floods came, and the wind blew, and burst against that house; and yet it did not fall, for it had been founded upon the rock. And everyone who hears these words of mine, and does not act upon them, will be like a foolish man, who built his house upon the sand. And the rain descended, and the floods came, and the wind is blew, and burst against that house; and it fell, and great was its fall." Matthew 7:24–27.

This is not a parable about one man who is saved in the other one lost. It's about two men who heard the word. We could even say it's a story about all of us. Notice the storm came to both men's houses, which is symbolic of their walk with God. Everything in this parable is the same except for one thing: one man heard the word but didn't act upon it. The result was total devastation of his house. The other man heard the Word and allowed faith to come, and then he acted on the Word, or what he heard. This man endured the storm of life. The word endure means to outlast. When the storm, or we could say sickness or any other attack, has come and gone, the man that heard and acted was still standing. James 1: 22–25 says,

"But prove yourselves doers of the word, and not merely hearers who delude themselves. For anyone is a hearer of the Word and not a doer, he is like a man who looks at his natural face in a mirror; for once he has looked at himself and gone away, he has immediately forgotten what kind of person he was. But one who looks intently at the perfect law, the law of liberty, and abides by it, not having become a forgetful hearer but effectual doer, this man shall be blessed in what he does."

The Word of God reflects the image of healing for which Jesus paid for on the cross. To hear the Word and not do it would be like be-holding your face in a mirror and then going off and forgetting what you look like in the natural. Anyone who forgets what he looks like has not spent enough time in front of a mirror. Spend time feeding on the promises of God until the image of God's healing provision is forever burned into your mind and spirit.

Now, I want you to go back to the beginning and read this book again. You couldn't possibly have gotten it all the first time. Repetition is an important part of the learning process.

CHAPTER FIFTEEN

TESTIMONY OF A BLIND EYE OPENED

"For we walk by faith and not by sight. This scripture took on a greater meaning for me when I awoke one morning blind in my right eye. Total blackness was all I saw in my right eye. Visits to doctors and specialists led to weeks, ending with carotid surgery. Throughout the darkness I know the Word promised my healing. "And by His stripes we are healed." (Isaiah 53:5) As the surgeon removed my bandages, he apologetically informed me that I would not regain sight in my right eye, and that my right eye would never see again! I politely informed him it is written: "But blessed are your eyes for they see. " (Matthew 13:16) Jesus healed the blind and He was going to heal me! I went up for healing during service. As I saw Pastor Brad spit on his hand, I was elated as I had seen this in my spirit. Pastor Brad placed the hand he had spit in on my right eye and prayed. When he removed his hand, I COULD SEE! My right eye vision was restored! PRAISE JESUS! A MIRACLE! Because of the carotid surgeries, I was required to follow up quarterly with sonograms to monitor for clots or blockages. A couple years later a scheduled sonogram revealed blood clots, LOTS of them. Pastor Brad announced that Father God wanted a Healing Service on a Certain date. I knew this was for me! I had not shared my test results with anyone, and these blood clots concerned me. During the healing service, I went up fully expecting to receive. For it is written: "All things are possible to him that believeth." (Mark 9:23) When Pastor Brad laid his hands on Both caryodid arteries, I felt FIRE! As he prayed the fire continued to burn in me! Without any medical proof, I knew I WAS HEALED! Insurance Approval finally came after this healing service for my CT scan. The results were NO BLOOD CLOTS! Thank You Jesus!

Now to a third miracle: at the age of 3 years old, my abuse/ molestation began. The confusion, isolation, fear, guilt, and shame continued to increase as I aged and become more aware of what was happening to me. My molestation lasted until I was 18, 15 years of torment. I cried out to Jesus! During a regular service at my church, His Image Ministries, Pastor Brad was teaching and suddenly off topic, asked if anyone had been abused? I RAN TO THE FRONT! Pastor Brad did not know my past, and yet he obeyed. As he laid hands on me and prayed, I knew my 50+ years of agony were finally over, PRAISE JESUSI Thank You Jesus! Thank you, Pastor Brad! I was EMOTIONALLY HEALED! No more flashbacks! NO MORE AGONY! NO MORE SHAME! The little girl in me was healed!!! I received MY miracle! It never occurred to me in all the years after accepting Jesus as my LORD, and SAVIOR, to ask for healing of the child within me. Jesus knew that broken child needed healing. Jesus wanted her healed! am so grateful for all the healings, miracles, and blessings I have received in my life. I am grateful that Jesus is my Lord and Savior, my Healer, my Provider, MY BEST FRIEND, and My Everything. I am so grateful for HIS WORD, HIS PROMISES and FAITH to receive. And I am so Thankful for my church and MY Pastor for His Obedience and his teachings on faith.

LET'S BELIEVE FOR YOUR HEALING

SAY THIS OUT LOUD - Father, in the name of Jesus, I speak and declare your healing provision over my body right now. I rebuke the curse of sickness and disease with the key of "binding" concerning that which I don't desire. I also call for your healing and miracle anointing to flow throughout my physical body and perfect a healing, and I cure within every cell and organ of my body. With the key of "loosening" I call for healing to flow into my body. I do not allow sickness the right to exist in my body and boldly proclaim that every disease, germ, and virus must bow its knee and die instantly in Jesus's name. I now release my faith in agreement with what you have said in Your Word. I now enter into rest and thank You that Your healing provision causes me to completely recover. I have now believed to receive the healing that Jesus bought and paid for with his own shed blood and having done all, I now stand firm in faith. From this moment forward, I will give you praise for that which I have believed to receive. Father God, I give you alone, all the glory, honor, and praise in Jesus' name. Amen.

www.ingramcontent.com/pod-product-compliance
Lightning Source LLC
Chambersburg PA
CBHW071112120626
46546CB00003B/1304